LAMBS & LILIES

MUSINGS OF LIKENESS REDEEMED AND
INNOCENCE RESTORED

RACHAEL CANNON

THE WRITER'S SOCIETY

LAMBS & LILIES

Musings of
Likeness Redeemed
And
Innocence Restored

A mystical, magical, and wildly imaginative devotional.

Rachael Cannon

ISBN:9781961180215

To contact the author, visit
Deliverance House Ministries at
www.deliverancehouseministries.org

Unless otherwise indicated, the Scripture quoted is taken from THE
MIRROR. Copyright © 2012.
Used with permission.

Cover designed in Canva.
Photo by themacx from Getty Images

TWS| The Writer's Society Publishing
Lodi, CA
www.thewriterssociety.online

❀ Created with Vellum

DEDICATION

For my loves
in county jails everywhere,
I've come to tell you how loved you are.

For Mandy
my sister and best friend,
A most beautiful incarnation of
other-centered love.

To Francois and Lydia du Toit,
in the light of the Mirror,
I have seen my original face
in the face of my Beloved.
Thank you for The Mirror Study Bible.

PREFACE

My darlings, I write with pleromic fingertips, dipped in rainbows, lacing my heart's words with gilded grace.

I tell of the all-embracing love of Abba in visions, prayers, allegories, reflective verse, and aphorisms in mystical prose and poetry.

Oh, my sweets, his love has deeply affected me.

My fingertips are full of God and oozing images of original likeness redeemed, innocence restored, inclusion, and effortless Union.

I shall attempt to outline Abba's dear face; read and see yourself in the mirror of his eyes.

Here, I shall dare to tell tales so vibrant and filled with love and life that any reader may easily be swept into

God's ecstatic and ever-loving embrace. May we come to know that we are the wonder of wonders.

These musings are Spirit-entwined, whispering, *I love you, I love you, I love you*, in every letter and reminding us that we have always been in Christ our Lovely Lord.

May they usher all into the awareness of Union and of our original likeness redeemed and blueprint innocence restored. Oh, that we are enraptured by unconditional love again and again.

I love you,

St. Rachael of the Lamb

1

LAMBS

LIKENESS REDEEMED

*The glory of God illuminates my life. The
Lamb is my lamp. The nations will
discover their redeemed likeness and
priceless value in the light of the Lamb
(REVELATION 21:26).*

The little lambs live in the Inner Land of Likeness, lovingly led to luscious green pastures by their gentle Shepherd. They live free and easy. Their tenderhearted Shepherd is a genius.

His cloak smells of sheepskins and pigpens, and hidden within are all mankind. He is lovely to be embraced, and so tender for all the little lambs to kiss with dry lips and be satiated by his sweet face forever.

. . .

THE LAMBS FRISK and play all day as the Shepherd pipes a lullaby of unconditional love. He soothes their hearts and mends their wounds with lovingkindness.

Merry is the flock in the luscious green pastures. The little lambs leap for no reason except that they are truly alive. They are dizzy with bliss and freedom.

HER FIRST LIFE breath was his. Newborn and newly shorn, he holds her face to face, nose to nose, forehead to forehead, and breath to breath. She sees the magical, lambent light of his love-filled eyes. And she grins all the wider.

> *She is finding her firm footing in the*
> *newfound freedom of her flawlessness*
> (GALATIANS 5:1).

The little lamb snuggles in and says, *Hold me.* He kisses her on the top of her head, and when he leans down, she smells his scent, intoxicating and magical.

It fills her. He smells like sheepskin and honeycomb. And the Shepherd replies,

Get lost in your darlingness to Me.

She feels scooped up and safe, and isn't afraid for the first time in a long time.

IS LIVING in likeness redeemed the ecstasy of Abba? Is this the crux of the message? As he is, so are we.

We are as blameless in this life as Jesus is!
(I JOHN 4:17).

It's the age of lambing, the age of likeness redeemed and innocence restored. The love of the Shepherd has overshadowed her fears, and she's forgotten them inside the warmth of his cloak.

Safely held in his love-soaked bosom, she finds the whole world. Sweetly, she smiles, a lambent child. Sweetly, she dreams of whispering streams.

SHE SEES the Firstling of the flock, the Lamb of God, who takes away the sins of the world. And she dotes on him.

THE LAMB CAME to reveal the likeness of God in human form. The Lamb has given birth to little lambs created in his image and likeness.

She delights in their likeness from sunup to moonset, and in the middle of the night, she grins.

She is pure and simple-hearted, brimming with innocence and the poetry of the pasture.

HER POTENTIAL ENAMORS HIM. He's molded the chaotic canvas of the little lamb's wanderings into a work of art.

. . .

THE CLERGY CONFINED the flock to a little artificial world of ceremonial, religious practices and pious extravaganzas, completely cut off from the reality of the wide-open pasture.

The tragedy of the pen is conformity and parameters. It keeps all the sheep sheared and confines them to a cell when there is a luscious green pasture that they were designed to graze.

The Shepherd is the gate, and the little lambs live like he has opened the gate for the world.

OH, she's Lamb-touched! Look at the smiles in her eyes, and she's giggling. She flutters when she walks, as if her feet aren't touching the ground.

MY DARLING little lambs
   You are indeed My kind,
   My kin, My likeness,
   My I-am-ness.
   Lamb in Lamb, I am.
   Identically, Plentifully Lamb, I am.
   With ravished ears, I hear his voice
   And know that I am lamb.
   So deep in Lamb, I am.
   I see into the life of things,
   Only Lamb light now.
   I am a wooly, white cloud.
   Drenched in kisses and

Held in utopian kindness.
Snow white lamb, I am.

NOTHING IS dearer in the universe to the Father, Son, and Holy Spirit than our likeness redeemed and innocence restored.

> *I pray that your thoughts will be flooded*
> *with likeness redeemed; that you will*
> *clearly picture his intent in identifying*
> *you in him so that you may know*
> *how precious you are to him. What*
> *God possesses in your redeemed inno-*
> *cence is his treasure and the glorious*
> *trophy of his inheritance. You are*
> *God's portion. You are the sum total of*
> *his assets and the measure of his*
> *wealth*
> *(EPHESIANS 1:18).*

Believe in your preciousness, Lambkin.
We are oh so precious to him.

Verdant and luxurious, refreshing and exhilarating, green and luscious, the plush grass is waving an invitation to lie down. The grass sings with no motive or expectation of reward.

We have no reason to wander, for all the greenest pastures are nearest to his house. Happy are the moments in the green, green meadow.

. . .

THE BEST PLACE TO enjoy effortlessness is where things grow. Go to the grassy green pasture. It will awaken your soul (Nachman of Bratzlav).

2

THE WONDERFUL WORLD OF IN

*I am in Christ by God's doing, not by
personal contribution
(1 Corinthians 1:30).*

Welcome to the Wonderful World of In. I've been gently placed here in Christ by the Father. Here I sit, high and In.

I see him. His whole face is light. He touched a finger to his chest, and that was that.

I knew I was In.

Wonder of wonders, I've been shown where God has placed us, and there is no one I cannot see here.

This wondrous world is delightful and sweet as if someone has tucked me into the center of Christmas.

He exists in all things and dwells in everyone. We live continuously, seamlessly, and consciously present in him, and he in us.

He is a womb, full of life and mystery and the weaving together of divinity and humanity. We are braided together in union, unmixed, and never separate.

OH, this Wonderful World of In! This is home. The Promised Land is not a geographical location. It is one new Incarnate Man that represents and embraces the entire human race.

It's a land of laughter, and the sweetness of being loved flows like honey. Rivers of the richest, most nutrient-filled milk flow from the breast of Abba, and all who drink are love-drunk.

My life force is strengthened in knowing I am In. Nothing can ever take that from me. I am in Christ, and Christ is in me.

> *Come to the conclusion for yourselves of his indwelling. Should it appear to you that Christ is absent in your life, look again; you have obviously done the test wrong*
> (2 CORINTHIANS 13:5).

The idea of separation has always been an illusion. We have never been separated, only in the abyss of a fallen mind.

Separation sickness creates all kinds of anxiety. Most suffering is from the illusion of separation. The illness of separation creates havoc on the mind.

> *So, now, with us awakening to our full*
>   *inclusion in this love union, everything*
>   *is perfect. This perfect love union is the*
>   *source of my confidence whenever we*
>   *face the scrutiny of contradictions*
> (*I JOHN 4:17*).

HOW INCLUDED YOU ARE, *my little lambs. If you only knew, you would not doubt. Lose the opinions of men and get to know Me for yourself.*

THE GOSPEL IS all about inclusion and affiliation – what a pity you should exclude someone sitting right next to you or even yourself. There is no us and them, only ALL. We are all included in Christ Jesus.

Them is US. We are ALL.

Grace is all-inclusive.

Humility comes from knowing we are all included.

There is no hierarchy. There are no levels.

We are all seated in one seat in the Risen Son.

> *Your master plan of inclusion is my medita-*
>   *tion (EPHESIANS 5:17).*

Oh, the bliss of inclusion; the Great In is such a relief from the pressure of competition.

We are all apostles of inclusion and Oneness.

3

LILIES

INNOCENCE RESTORED

*She was given the finest linen wherewith
she clothed herself; there she stands,
wrapped in radiant white - dressed in
spotless, saintly innocence. (This innocence gives testimony to the merits of
the Redeemer)*
(REVELATION 19:8).

S he stands before him in immaculate innocence
and spotless magnificence because of the work
Christ finished on the cross.

Nothing can be added to or taken from what Christ
has already done.

*It finally dawned on her that no contribu-
tion from her side could possibly add to
what God has already accomplished*
(ROMANS 4:19).

This gave her an immediate sense of freedom to enjoy being so loved.

> *But now, wow! Everything has changed;*
> *you have discovered yourselves to be*
> *located in Christ. What once seemed so*
> *distant is now so near. His blood reveals*
> *your redeemed innocence and authentic*
> *genesis (EPHESIANS 2:13).*

The blood that surged through her veins could not wait to tell her who she was. She feasts on sustained innocence, sustained without objection. It is original, continual, and has no interruption.

Aware of her innocence, she enjoys the Trinity residing within. She lives abandoned among the snow-white lilies, face to face in blameless innocence with Abba.

There is no shadow of shame to darken her face. She realizes Abba's manifest embrace in and around her. She is safe. She is In. She is innocent.

> *So now, just like an infant in a mother's*
> *embrace, abide in this place of inno-*
> *cence where his manifest appearance is*
> *meant to be fully realized and echoed in*
> *unashamed utterance! In his immediate*
> *presence, there exists no sense of shame*
> *or separation (1 JOHN 2:28).*

She is mostly in infant mode, abiding in His embrace in the place of innocence. She smiles and giggles and wiggles a little.

Oh, the sweetness of this preserved and redeemed innocence. How can it be? Our conversation no longer dwells on sin-consciousness, only innocence restored.

> *Beloved when we know what God knows to*
> *be true about us, then instead of*
> *condemning us, our hearts will endorse*
> *our innocence and free our conversation*
> *before God (1 JOHN 3:21)*

In her hair, she wears a lily-of-the-valley flower crown. Abba calls her *Perfect*. She is sweet, beautiful, and innocent.

She grows towards him. She's a heliotropic lily, and his approval is the Son.

He never reminds her of a blemished past. He reminds her she has no wrinkle, stain, residue, or remainder of sin.

Nothing has carried over from old Adam.

WHILE YOU WERE SLEEPING, I bathed you from every accusation and opinion that was not Mine.

I anointed you with My very breath and sealed you from the inside out before you were even formed.

Remember your innocence before Adam?

That's the innocence I restored!

I've released you from every word spoken in judgment, anger, suspicion, and doubt from your own mind and your brothers.

If you must compare yourself, then compare yourself to the lilies; they neither toil nor spin and are clothed in the radiance of innocence.

They lean their heads on my breast.

I sustain them and make them lovely.

> *Standing free and forgiven in their*
> *redeemed innocence and union, face to*
> *face before the Throne of God, they are*
> *fully engaged, day and night, in their*
> *priestly service of worship in the inner*
> *sanctuary. The One seated upon the*
> *Throne is their tabernacle – he shelters*
> *them with his presence*
> *(REVELATION 7:15).*

I have cleared you. I covered you. I dressed you in My own robes. You are clean because of My Word spoken in you from the inside out.

You are clean because of Love's conversation to include all of humanity in Our Love.

I DID ALL this without your permission.

. . .

I DID it all without you asking Me.

I DID it all so you would never feel unclean or not good enough for our relationship.

THERE IS no darkness in you, Abba whispers.

4

MY DARLING DAUGHTER

The most significant title in the world is *Daughter.*

ENJOY BEING MY DAUGHTER.

Ever loved and always wanted My daughter of divine wisdom, the bliss of the Beloved, in you rests the whole Trinity, the whole Truth, and nothing but the Truth.

I FEEL LOVED in the core of my being. Like I'm held together by perfect love.

I intuitively know how to be a daughter. You don't have to tell a flower to bloom. You don't have to tell me how to behave. I instinctively know how to be me.

The only title that can contain me is Daughter.

· · ·

BEHOLD, I have well named you, Made-of-Me.

I WAS BORN full of God. I'm embellished and adorned with love so special and intimate, and delighted in abundantly.

I'm Your darling baby, Your heart, Your dream, Your delight, and I know it!

DO you know what you mean to Me, My Daughter?

I delight to do you good. To lavish you with every heavenly blessing is bliss for Me.

Congratulations on being great!

I'm so excited about your life, My Darling Daughter.

I FEEL MORE myself than ever. Free to be me, and it's beautifully uncomplicated. Designed to glow, glitter, gleam, shine, and radiate, I'm decked out in the red roses of ardent love.

The love of my Abba causes me to rise above and beyond reason and logic.

With a smiling heart, I see him within me.

The same heart of love that created the world loves me uniquely, individually, and personally. He unconditionally enfolds his children in love.

· · ·

I HAVE the reflection of his face in my skin and the illumination of his unveiled existence in my eyes, like a twinkle.

I'm glowing from knowing the tender affection of my Abba.

I'M WARM, like sitting beside a bonfire on a cold wintery night. The warmth draws people and makes them feel cherished.

He's a burning fire in the marrow memory of my bones. Softly and sweetly, and tenderly, I burn.

MY FACE IS alight with wonder and curiosity. I smell of honey and rain.

I am luminous and full of secret visions.

I KNOW NO RITUAL WORDS, but I know what's written in my heart. I've heard Love's conversation to include the world in Their relationship.

The future is hidden here, in my heart, simple and eternal, and one breath at a time.

Death at my back, life in front of and within me, every step has always been a step into Abba's dream of Union and inclusion.

He so loves the world. And I do, too.

I am, I AM's daughter.

. . .

YOU ARE the daughter I've always wanted, the light of My days.

You look radiant. And oh, how you've grown.

HIS EYES GIVE SO MUCH AWAY. He overwhelms my feelings of lessness with moreness. I swear my eyes have turned into little hearts.

I live permanently in his presence, for he is within me.

GOOD MORNING,
My darling,
My lambkin,
My kin,
My kind,
My own,
My delight,
My joy,
My mirror-image,
My likeness,
My I-am-ness.
Enjoy My love. Enjoy the ride.
Enjoy your flight. Enjoy My tender affection.
You are My daughter, and I am more than pleased with you.
Your company is My treasure.
I love you here (he taps his fingertips to his chest).
Abba

5

RAINBOW MEET FEET

I met a girl named Rainbow on 2/3/23 in Birmingham, Alabama. She tapped me on the shoulder and smiled.

HER FATHER, Matt Spinks, preached the Gospel; the message of Christ's finished work of the cross. His smiling Rainbow assured me that Christ did it all.

I SEE A RAINBOW-COLORED WORLD. I fly through grace-colored rainbows.

A RAINBOW FOR FOOTING, My love, and rest from flying from time to time.

.   .   .

THERE'S no place like home.

There's no place like home.

There's no place like home.

MYSTERIES REQUIRE flexible minds and lots of rainbows.

I've got rainbow keys for typing. I'm writing from inside a pot of gold, and rainbow words flow out with life and love.

I smile in wonder at the rainbow garden in my heart. It's vibrant and full of grace that speaks of Abba's love in every color.

WHERE DO rainbows grow wild and in all shapes and sizes? Where can you pick rainbows like wildflowers? Where do troubles melt like lemon drops?

I've discovered the birthplace of all the rainbows ever in the world. Only one place I know.

In Abba, The Wonderful World of In.

HIGH HERE,

Take wind walks!
High, high,
Heaven's lips,
Kiss, kiss, kiss.
Life kissed lips.

· · ·

FLYING HIGH,
> *High life.*
> *In pure ecstasy.*
> *Swirl, swirl.*
> *Twirl, twirl.*
> *Ah, rapturous is His love.*

WINDSONG SWEET,
> *Rainbow meets feet.*
> *Look!*
> *Safe and secure*
> *From all alarms.*

STANDING ON A RAINBOW NOW.
> *High here*
> *Life kissed lips.*
> *Oh, rapturous Love.*

HE HAS PLACED us here to see from this privileged position, which is not a height reserved for the elect but a solid platform for everyone as they know his arms.

HIS IS a cloak of every color, and hidden inside is a multi-colored rainbow of humankind.

. . .

1 Wʜᴀᴛ ᴀ ꜰᴇʟʟᴏᴡꜱʜɪᴘ,
    What a joy divine
    Leaning on the everlasting arms
    What a blessedness,
    What a peace is mine.
    Leaning on the everlasting arms.

Rᴇꜰʀᴀɪɴ:
    Leaning, leaning,
    Safe and secure from all alarms.
    Leaning, leaning
    Leaning on the everlasting arms.

2 Oʜ, *how sweet to walk in this pilgrim way,*
    Leaning on the everlasting arms.
    Oh, how bright the path
    Grows from day to day,
    Leaning on the everlasting arms.

3 Wʜᴀᴛ ʜᴀᴠᴇ *I to dread,*
    What have I to fear,
    Leaning on the everlasting arms?
    I have blessed peace,
    With my Lord so near
    Leaning on the everlasting arms.
    (E.A. Hoffman, 1887).

6

RICH IN LIVING SILENCE

*Our accurate hearing is what distinguishes
us as the resurrection generation. Hear
what the Father is saying about the life
of our design (1 PETER 1:14).*

R ich, she is in warm, living silence.
A world of profound beauty and peace emerges in the spaciousness of silence and solicitude.

In the silence, she learned another form of language. Beyond the surface, she watches with her heart, not her eyes. She hears, though not with ears.

Listening has become life, and she has the King's ear. Her ears hold words.

TO HEAR, one must be silent.
Wide-eyed listening looks like savoring, relishing,

reveling, enjoying, appreciating, immersing, and soak-
ing. In the Selah moments, we pause, reflect, and enjoy
living in Union with God.

SHE HEARS WHO PEOPLE ARE. She knows the language of
hearts.

So many people are trying to tell you about things
that don't matter. Some people talk so much that they
never stop to listen.

JESUS SENT his word (love's conversation) and healed a
young man in another city. So, she's experimenting
with ways to send messages across long distances.

She listens beyond her years and ears, through
earth and air, past time and space, and skin and
sinews. She can hear the brook whispering over the
rocks, the waves sighing his name, the sparrows
singing, and the liveliness of plants.

She listens and hears the world crying. She listens
and hears Abba's heartbeat within their cry. He is
filling every nook and cranny with his love.

IN THE SOLITUDE, she realized she had never been
alone. Although it is silent, it is far from dull.

For the first time in her life, there is no nagging in
her soul, no contrary voices to wholeness. She is
bound to I Am, and this sense of belonging is ecstasy.

.   .   .

WHEN SHE SEES HIM, she sees what she thought was lost was not lost at all, but all was wholly found. His face has no lines of worry, only joy and assurance. She looks at him, and love fills her. The energy of Their love fills the silence like invisible waves of joy and light and laughter.

She puts her hand over her mouth, but a giggle escapes and breaks the silence. She used to be frightened and full of mountains until his smile melted her fears.

IN THE STILLNESS, in the quiet no-thing-ness, she is grounded in Union. In the blissful awareness that we are One is a gloriously entangled life to be lived. Sitting in the silence, we see all that Christ accomplished.

HOLD YOUR TONGUE, for God's sake, and let her enjoy being so loved and loving the world. If you must break the silence, then,

> Soak your hearing in thoughts that bring
>   flavor to every conversation
> (LUKE 14:35).

> Habitually fine-tune your ears to always

resonate with the voice of likeness within. Don't become a worry addict! Never ever allow the anxieties of the physical world to intoxicate you and overload you with distractions
(LUKE 21:34).

7

CASALI DEL PINO

THE CHANTING FIELDS

*My most beautiful grain of wheat, heart of
my heart. In your death, you produced
much fruit (JOHN 12:24).*

T he world is full of God. The whole world is
overflowing with the expression of divine fecun-
dity (Pierre Teilhard de Chardin).

A SINGLE GRAIN has become a world of chanting fields
full of pearls and treasures. Every creature echoes,
pictures, and mirrors the image and likeness of the
Trinity.

OH, my lovely, lovely grain of wheat. You have made us
perfect sons. Thank you, my darling Son, my Jesus, my

Lamb, my lovely grain of wheat. The field of the world is ripe and ready for harvest.

One Incorruptible and fecund Seed has produced all.

THE CHILDREN of the field chant of their belonging. They sing songs from My Right Hand, My Eastern Seat, My Risen Son, and My Pleasure forevermore.

They chant paternal songs in a manner that delights Abba, Father. He is fond of the chanting fields.

OUR SONG SOARS into the night air, so strident you can see the notes winding their way through the fields of grain. Blissed chants resonate, packed with power to cross miles at the speed of light and two trillion galaxies of stars.

We chant lullabies to the slow pulse of redeemed blood, sing songs to scare away lessness, and weave rhymes to remind us how Abba knit our flesh together.

We chant and see invisible fields. The fields of energy and light are woven together, *pleko*, braided, plaited, created, and bound by divine love and life.

We chant and see our Seed's face in every living being. All matter is pregnant with God.

OUR UNION IS a dialect of heartbeats strung together

with the lilt of other-centered love and the blessed assurance of eternal togetherness.

It sounds absurd, but the rhythm of it is easy and familiar. No need to think about the words. They fill our mouths and spill over like water out of a cup. The sound of our songs becomes a stream made to carry the melody of life along.

The world is the well that never runs dry.

We sing psalms in a language without words and find ourselves falling into the Birthday song. We sing about the Incarnation and of living forever with Abba.

CHRIST HAS INTERWOVEN his Life throughout the world. By him and through him, all things are created. The world is braided with God-DNA.

OH, *the bliss of the chanting fields,*
Hear us sing?
Oh, how sweet our Incorruptible Seed,
The Seed who was planted in all.
Oh, how sweetly the field knows the Seed.
We sing of our sweet Seed.
Oh, how sweet and lovely You are,
Most fecund grain of wheat.

8

THE TABLE

Your every meal makes the mandate of his
coming relevant and communicates the
meaning of the New Covenant
(1 Corinthians 11:26).

They say that no matter how many sit at this table, there is always room for more. The whole point of communion is to be gathered together in love.

From now on, our meals are meaningful. We celebrate that the Incarnation reveals our redemption; the promise became a Person.

Whether you eat or drink, you are declaring
your joint inclusion in his death and
resurrection, confirming your redeemed
innocence (1 Corinthians 11:25-26
Commentary, Francois du Toit).

Smell the scent of Risen Bread coming from the royal bakery? See the long, low feast tables lining the king's palace, golden in the festive lamplight?

A CELEBRATION HAS BEEN PREPARED for us, and feasting is highly recommended. All are welcome at the feast of fellowship and the communion of Union.

We celebrate the success of the cross.

The Lamb is all done!

I HEAR the clamor of sumptuous celebrations and the voices of anointed ones celebrating their I-am-ness with the Risen Lamb, our delectable Bread of Life.

Every meal is a memory of our communion. Every meal becomes a reminder of Union. His body was broken for all.

Enjoy the banquet feast of Union and inclusion.

PEOPLE SEIZED with panic come to the table for warm bread and peace. People without community come and find fellowship. People with no exits come to the table and find a way out. Love has a way of making empty bellies overflow.

The Chef says, *Get ready to be romanced. I know the way to your heart.*

.   .   .

EVERY MEAL REMINDS me that the Incarnation has happened in me. We are One. I enjoy this inseparable and effortless Union like a never-ending feast.

OH, my honey-eyed butter roll, my seared scallops in red curry, my delicious raspberry sorbet, Jesus.

The least little thought of you and my soul is inflamed with Love.

WHEN I GAZE ON HIM, *all sadness and need are snatched away from me so that I have the manners of a simple little girl and not that of an old woman* (Hildegard of Bingen).

I DRINK the wine of the New Covenant, and the last of my discomfort vanishes, replaced by a warm flutter. The warmth in my chest spreads to my veins as if I were drunk on love.

JESUS SITS at the table with the persons that religion abhors. Leave your religious sentiment behind and enjoy the feast of Union.

9

ANOUTHEN MEMORIES
BORN ABOVE

No one can fully engage in heaven's
perspective unless one's heavenly origin
is realized. The Son of Man declares
mankind's co-genesis from above
(JOHN 3:13).

No one is unbegun, and all mankind originates from above. We all began in God.

It was his delightful resolve to give birth to
us; we were conceived by the unveiled
logic of God. We lead the exhibition of
his handiwork, like first fruits
(JAMES 1:18).

Born from above in love, the world has no hold on her. She was molded and formed by love from above.

We are Same-kind, God-kind; like words entwined in poetry, our thoughts are co-elevated with his thoughts.

> *If your life was a product of the world*
> *system, you would enjoy their applause*
> *and friendship; but because you've*
> *discovered your authentic identity in*
> *My declaration of who you are by*
> *design, their mold no longer has any*
> *hold on you (JOHN 15:19).*

MY MEMORIES RETURN from being born above, reminding me of who I have always been. By the soft glow of Sonlight, the world awakens to the unassailable assurance of anouthen memories.

The Trinity sang us all into being. In the beginning, we were a love song, and the songs had the power of love. They sang a love song for every human, and it was accompanied by Triune dancing.

Abba sings a song our bones remember, and we wake up and live.

Memory, you are full to the brim of God and plunged into the depths of divine love from above.

FATHER'S WORDS found us in the black, in the dark, blindfolded by the fallen mind. His voice brought his face into perfect view. When he sang, something deep inside awakened, and our eyes opened as if we had been sleeping.

He calls us by name, *Child*.

SOMETHING SHIFTS DEEP WITHIN, imbuing us with a sense of Oneness as though we have finally connected to some vital part of ourselves, and we take shape. The love abounding in His sole paternity gives us form and portion.

His voice runs through the world like a pleasant stream, soothing and comforting, reminding us that we have always been born from above.

> *Everyone who realizes their association in him, convinced that he is their original life and that his name defines them, God gives the assurance that they are indeed his offspring, begotten of him; he sanctions the legitimacy of their sonship (JOHN 1:12).*

> *These are the ones who discover their genesis in God, beyond their natural conception... You are indeed the greatest idea that God has ever had (JOHN 1:13).*

The sound of his voice calms thoughts of separation. His love words bathe us like newborn babes and remind us that we are his own.

.　.　.

You know the Voice that formed you.

Union is your only way out.

If you must escape due to hurt or heartache, escape into Me, within you.

Get lost in Union. We are effortlessly one.

Here, I will cause you to remember who you are and where you come from.

Oh, Divine Genesis

Oh, bosom beginning.

Abba is a frenzy of love for me.

I can never be separated from Love.

Your love transcends beyond my earthly beginning and end.

I am ecstatic. Agape is my Father, and I am rich in love.

I hear your heartbeat for me, and it puts me in motion, in perichoresis steps learned in the womb before the world's foundation (Eugene Peterson).

10

BE YOUR BLOOD

The blood of Jesus was not different from the blood of any other person. If there was some mysterious power in the blood of Jesus, then all we needed was a blood transfusion.

What makes his blood most powerfully significant is what it communicates.

In the broken, bleeding body of Jesus, the Incarnate Engineer of the universe willingly dies humanity's death at the hands of his own creation in order to redeem our minds from the plague of sin-consciousness that left us distanced and indifferent. (Francois du Toit).

HE HAS TETHERED himself to me in the core of my life force. Fit is the blood flowing through my veins.

It is Life. My blood is threaded with gold and crimson brighter than mortal blood and suffused with a sweet honey fragrance.

Oh, the power of life and healing in his blood. His blood communicates our unstained innocence like we've only dreamt of.

THE HEALTH-GIVING DRAUGHT *that I drink deeply of is the blood of Jesus* (Mechtild of Magdeburg).

DO YOUR WOUNDS STILL HURT? Christ asked.

He leaned forward, taking my hand. The warmth of his love flooded my body like warm blood, healing the last of my energies and replenishing the well in my soul that had sunk dangerously low. I breathed easier, and the strength returned to my limbs.

He is a Man brimming with compassion and life. His story is now mine, carried in my underskin river of royal lineage.

THE BLOOD that runs through my veins reminds me who I am. It is the wine of the New Covenant, and I am the fruit of the Vine.

There is no liquid created, which he likes to give us so much. It is so plentiful and carries and shares our authentic likeness redeemed and innocence restored.

Sticky love, like myrrh, aged and oozing, gooey and sappy, filled my pores and sank into the marrow of my bones and soul. It permeates in me a sweet aroma. Gummy-like resin, I can't shake it. It's touched me. It absorbs my whole life. I'm thickly coated in Abba's love, and it's seeped into every fiber of my being. This love is gluey, clingy, viscous, and tenacious. The color of love is blood and honey.

THIS BLOOD GIFT has been passed down from generation to generation since the cross of Christ. The blood of the New Covenant swells in my veins, upsetting 2000 years of tradition and setting me free to be me.

I hear his voice, and my blood begins to sing.

Awake, Awake, and remember the first light of God's face at my birth.

Held together from the inside out by unconditional love, likeness redeemed, and innocence restored. The myrrh fills every room in my temple. The blood speaks and reminds me of our sweet Union.

> *Your original identity is defined by what*
> *God, the Father of mankind, has always*
> *cherished about you; how your pre-*
> *Adamic innocence would be preserved*
> *in the prophetic word and redeemed*
> *through the obedience of Jesus Christ*
> *and the effect of the sprinkling of his*
> *blood. Realizing his grace and peace*
> *exceed any definition of contradiction or*
> *reward (1 Peter 1:2).*

11

UTOPIAN EMBRACE

I accommodate myself in God's delight,
yielding in awe to his firm embrace. I
make myself at home in his delight
(HEBREWS 12:28B).

O h, love, love, hold me fast.
     I have thee close, My Dearest Darling.
     Hold me one moment longer.
Peace, My Darling, peace,
Thou was meant chiefly to delight
(Mechtild of Magdeburg).

I AM HOLDING onto Thee for dear Life.

I used to hold him because I was afraid. I'd run to
him and hide in his utopian embrace, locked in tender
love. In his arms, my fear dissolved.

Now, I run to him for cuddles and hold him for affection. I enjoy his warmth and love.

ENJOY MY STRONGHOLD, My Darling Daughter.

I'M ENGULFED in the utopian arms of the most adorable Majesty of the Father, Son, and Holy Spirit.

> *I snuggle up in the comfort of his intimate embrace (2 CORINTHIANS 1:4).*

He takes me up in himself and hides me in his arms. I behold the Creator of the world. I'm in his arms, yet he is inside of me.

Ah, for God's sake, how can this be?

I EMBRACE all blossoming life within myself in this utopian tenderness.

IN MY HEART, He is and dwells in heaven. I am heaven. You are heaven (St. Symeon the New Theologian).

AH, this love-inspired hug-hold is taking me from Old to New. From law to grace... In his arms, a radical mind shift takes place.

· · ·

LOCKED IN HIS EMBRACE, I have an Aha Moment, and I remember that I've always been held.

You've held me until I remembered who I am.

He upholds the life of my design
(HEBREWS 12:9).

He has my ultimate wellness in mind. I can rest assured in his upholding. Oh, the uphold! I am held in co-elevated arms.

When he holds me, warmth blooms inside of me. He slips through the wall around my heart and is all the love I have ever wished for.

The last of my discomfort vanishes, replaced by a warm flutter. The warmth in my chest spreads to my thoughts as if I were drunk on wine.

I YIELD to his firm embrace and accommodate myself to his delight. I feel an ineffable and utopian tenderness, and I am blissed. I have always been held in the everlasting joy of all eternity.

I forget illusions of separation and distance. I have never not been held.

HERE I AM, cradled in the warm, utopian embrace of Abba, it's Paradise. Every precious moment, Your arms eternally engulf me. Knowing Abba's arms are upholding me causes me to deeply enjoy every moment.

I BREATHE IN, and I'm aware of Your upholding arms. This is how I enjoy being so loved: a smile, a giggle, a tremor, a tear. I stop all my wiggling to be held.

All my days, I've been saved. Before the world's foundation was laid, I was saved. I've always been safe and secure in Abba's arms.

YOUR UNCREATED HANDS have done everything for me. You have given me everything. You nourish my heart. The satisfaction of your utopian embrace is sublime, wonderful, and inconceivable.

I ponder redemption realities from these co-seated arms. My heart's pockets hold thoughts of likeness redeemed and innocence restored for pondering.

MY HEART FLUTTERS with love so intense I could disintegrate, but I'm not afraid to become nothing in his arms. This feeling is quite the opposite of fear. It's sheer ecstasy.

Love's arms are holding me in heavenly places, and he's beaming. He likes holding me.

· · ·

I'M CURRENTLY CUDDLED in sweetness, with tears of love drenching my head like oil running down his beard. I am rocked like a child by our Great Father in whose arms I have awoken. I have always been held.

Far from the toil and my overly intense activity, I've been cradled and caressed and kissed until I awoke and succumbed to being like a child in the arms of God. I've been held all along. I've just awoken.

MY GREAT ABBA of easy-won happiness and intoxication upholds me. Oh, the uphold is grand! I sink into a feeling of security that I've realized before. His arms eternally protect me.

Hot tears spring to my eyes as these caresses warm my soul. Immediately, I feel bathed in the Son, expressing an effortless Union that words never could. I close my eyes and hold him back!

I HEAR HIM SING, *Me, Mine. You're in Me, and I'm in you.*
   You are Mine, and I am yours.
   Mine, all Mine.

HE CLUTCHES me to his chest and steals every terror and abuse I've ever had, not denying they didn't happen but smothering the flames of fear with something greater: arms of absolute love and blessed eternal assurance.

It feels utopian and euphoric. How can this be? He touches his chest to remind me where I've come from. He pulls me into a tight embrace and cradles my head against his shoulder, where I remain for a long time.

PEACE FILLS my soul and pulses to his heartbeat. Light twinkles in my eyes, and I glitter a little. He sets his sights on me and enfolds me again, time and again, time and again.

SI FORTE ATTRECTENT EUM – If they hold him tightly, they shall see Him rightly. The secret is that he is holding us.

EUPHORIA AND ECSTASY ENGULF ME. I am deeply engulfed in the layers of Your divine omnipresence. The universal and enveloping embrace of the Trinity has won me. Never a moment have I not been engulfed in Your utopian embrace, no, not one. No, not one.

HERE, I am nourished and revitalized. The arms made for enfolding stretch out wide for me. I am a Tree hugger clinging tightly to the Tree of Life, the life of all life that holds me now, even as I type.

12

MON TRESOR

I t is you. You are my pearl of delight.
Mon Tresor, My Treasure.

As with all rare things of great value, attention to detail is essential. High-valued pearls require much kissing and affection.

She sees the keeper of the Imperial Treasury. He is a kind man, covered in vibrant feathers, and he carries a speaking pearl in his bosom, which he stops to take out and kiss every few paces.

She can tell from how he adores the pearl and holds

it close with great affection it is his most prized possession.

WE'RE deep in the Imperial Treasury of the bright palace, being treasured and doted on here.

THE TREASURE of love is made known to me. What a treasure You are, what a gift You are, Jesus. Your love is the greatest treasure of my life, and You treasure us with great affection.

O' You treasure, immeasurable in your fullness! Mon Tresor.

I AM SUCH a treasure that he hides me in the safest place, himself. He is the Imperial Treasurer. He holds the wealth of the world inside of himself. We are the sum total of all his assets, his prime investments.

I AM YOUR SAFE-KEEPER. I am your sweet assurance.
I will protect you. I always have. I always will.
You are safe in my arms.
Now go have fun.
Enjoy the safety of My love.

· · ·

He LONGS for me to know my value. He longs for me to know I'm safe.

Ah, sweet love of mine,
   Oh, my tenderhearted, gentle Lord.
   I am satiated in your love.
   Full, fuller, fullest of love,
   The treasure of your love is my delight.
   This rich and hidden treasure is within.
   I take out this pearl of most preciousness, and I kiss it.
You, my greatest treasure; immeasurable in value and preserved in innocence (Mechtild of Magdeburg).

13

THE DIVINE MILIEU

Christ is all and in all
(COLOSSIANS 3:11, Amplified Bible, Classic
   Edition).

Through your Incarnation, my God, all matter is henceforth incarnation (Pierre Teilhard de Chardin).

THE DIVINE MILIEU is the environment of Union.

I feel a smile spreading across my face as I consider the implications of Union. All things are divine. I see the Trinity in everything. This becomes the Source of my delight and enjoyment in creation and human beings.

Namaste, indeed. I see Christ in you; do you in me see Thee?

. . .

MY EYES ARE enlightened and aware of the Divine Milieu. The world is full of God. He has chosen the world to express and diffuse his presence and influence in everything. That's love!

CHRIST, *as the Incarnation of God, is in matter, life, and energy. He is the life, the matter, the energy of all. This pervasive Divine presence is at work at all levels of human and geological activity, animating and directing the web of relationships. He is all and is in all* (Pierre Teilhard de Chardin).

MY FAITH IS Incarnational and Christocentric. My seeing is experienced through the senses, in touching and tasting. I savor that which nourishes my inner perception of the fullness of God in all things.

THE PRESENCE *of the Incarnate Word penetrates everything. It shines at the common heart of things as the Center that is infinitely intimate to them* (Pierre Teilhard de Chardin).

EVERYTHING around me has become the substance of Your heart! I see Your face in every face. I see Your face in every flower.

· · ·

THE INCARNATE COSMOS is the incarnate world in which I see the Union of God and mankind in all things. He has brought two worlds together inseparably. He incarnates every cell and microbe that makes up the entire world.

YOUR UNIVERSAL PRESENCE is the all-inclusive center on which everything is gathered. I can only preach the mystery of You in everything. You are in all, and You are all (Pierre Teilhard de Chardin).

THE DIVINE MILIEU is my surrounding environment in which I see all God and flesh have become One. This Union is the milieu from which I see myself, others, and the world. Here, there is no us and them, only All.

LIFE, to me, is a sure sign of Love in the Divine Milieu. I enjoy, with smiles and sighs, love experienced in new ways in the light of the Divine Milieu.

The power of his love animates all energy. He unites and completes all beings within his breast. The power of love unleashed at the resurrection still surges through the universe.

The Divine love of Abba is materializing and energizing the world; it's all-consuming and enveloping all.

. . .

THE MARVEL of the Divine Milieu is that we are all *participating in living, moving, and having our being in God. In this ocean of life, everything is divinized, divinizing, and divinizable* (Pierre Teilhard de Chardin).

IN LIGHT OF THIS DISCOVERY, I shall resume my exploration through the inexhaustible wonders of humanity and creation, which the Divine Milieu has in store for me. I look for my Abba's face in every face, and if I cannot see him, I shall look again and again until I do.

(EXCERPTS FROM *THE DIVINE MILIEU*, Pierre Teilhard de Chardin).

14

THE HURT

*People must feel safe in your conversation;
therefore, slander and hurtful words are
out! Be inspired by kindness and
compassion (see EPHESIANS 4:31-32).*

The hurt was marrow-deep and in a place that only love could reach.

I had learned to guard my thoughts so well that I was almost afraid of what they were.

No amount of prayer, warfare, praise, or memorization helped to soothe my aching soul. I casted out, and I did the binding and loosing. I chanted, praised, and shakabaka'd. And I still hurt.

THERE IS no love in rituals, principles, or fundamentals. Being held beats doing warfare.

. . .

OTHERS SAID, *Don't get bitter, read the Bait of Satan, stay plugged in, get to the root, examine your ways, dig through your past, renounce and break all generational patterns, cut soul ties, fast, and pray in the Spirit real loud.*

When I was crying in my bed, I whispered *Help, Hold me.*

LOVE IS a Man with warm arms and a chest meant to be laid on. His heartbeat is meant to be felt and heard. He knows deep wounds. He knows deeper still how to heal them. He holds me, and the hurt lessens, a little at first. I like being held and nuzzled by Love.

The more I'm held, the less my heart hurts.

IN HIS ARMS, I feel my wounds growing new skin. My newborn skin sparkles a little. It's still tender where I was stoned.

I remember the stoning with a new understanding. It wasn't just the religious elders who led the stone assault. I stoned myself, too.

The stones of adversity flew in my mind from believing less than what Abba believed about me. Being held changed my mind and healed my hurt.

Oh, the bliss of being stoned! I got stoned.

It changed my life. It changed my mind!

· · ·

IF YOU'VE EVER LIVED a lie, living the truth, once you've found it, is even sweeter (Joy D'Arcy, The Mirror Word Bible Study Group, Facebook).

WORDS OF A FALLEN IDENTITY, a DIY mentality, were like hunting dogs that tracked me down, nipped at my heels, and mauled me. My mind was in a continual state of accusation and condemnation. My heart hurt. I needed to believe something different.

WHERE ARE YOUR ACCUSERS NOW? (see JOHN 8:3-11).

Listen to Me, Darling Daughter, and you won't have to fend for yourself. Take sides with Me. Believe what I believe about you.

I will always take care of you. I will never leave you hurt, rejected, or exposed.

I'll protect you and heal you.

I am your safeguard.

I hear your heart. Can you hear Mine?

I will not harm you. I will keep you safe.

I love you just the way you are.

Don't be so quick to cut away pieces of yourself, incessantly editing who you are to fit in. If you edit yourself, you'll edit others.

SLANDER, teasing, and hurtful words are out. He reminds us of how deeply we are adored. He holds me, and I am healed. I used to be frightened and full of mountains, but his stronghold soothed my cares.

As my wounds healed and my mind cleared, I became a healer.

PEOPLE COME to me for safety in conversation. I'm inspired by kindness and compassion. I bonded with the Man of lovingkindness who shared his heart with me. I am a safe place where people don't wear masks or steal little pieces of each other away.

I don't recommend formulas, steps, or warfare. I suggest savoring what his Stronghold feels like in the depths of your soul. I recommend enjoying long walks and delighting in being so loved.

I LIVE ABANDONED and healed among the white lilies, and the night is under my feet. My mind and heart fly in the land of laughter as I sit on a footstool and stare at the Lover and Healer of humanity.

Our darlingness is important to Abba. Our emotional wellness is dear to him. He is very fond of us, and we have a special place in him. Find your spot. He loves us more than just a little.

MANY OF US go through life feeling slightly broken and alone, surrounded all the time by others who feel exactly the same way. Abba tucks us under his arm and whispers, *We are in this together. You are not alone. You are beautiful to Me.*

He has placed a value on our lives that is beyond dispute. We are irreducible.

HE IS EMMANUEL, and God is with us. If we must relive the hurtful memories, we see Abba is with us. He is in every detail. His love takes the sting out, and here he is with us in the pain.

I DON'T BELIEVE the caustic lies I once did. I don't do warfare anymore. I've found a greater reality nestled under Abba's wing and living on his chest. Don't worry about the warfare. No need to shakabaka or break soul ties.

Psst, You have always been in an unbreakable bond with Me. I am your soul tie. No need to tear down strongholds. Just enjoy The Stronghold of My Arms. Oh, that you would know what I know about you, darling. Let Me change the way you see yourself, and when you see yourself, you will see the world!

(FOR FURTHER INSIGHT, *Rainy Day Women #12 & 35*, Bob Dylan, YouTube.)

15

FLIGHT IN FAITH

*If it seems that someone continues to antici-
pate their next failure (by carrying just
too much load) from your position in
faith, restore such a person in a spirit of
courtesy and grace, keeping your own
attitude in check; a legalistic approach
would want to suspiciously probe into
problems (GALATIANS 6:1).*

She has a history of imagination. In the
beginning, before she remembered her
anouthen genesis, she suffered from the imagination of failure and lessness. She had flights of
failure.

She remembers the imagination of lessness. She
had been sitting like an empty eggshell, hollow and
chest-heavy. Back before Abba removed her blindfold
and gave her a bite of bread.

．　．　．

WASHED IN HIS LOVE, he flushed her cloudy eyes with pure light and gave her mind wings. He took her on a flight in faith and seated her in Love's arms with the rest of the world.

FANTASY ISN'T wishful thinking but a way of reflecting on reality. She thinks of a realer realm than she can see with earth eyes. She grins as she sees. Her face hints of a Union beyond which no scholar has ever seen or written about. Living by faith now, it made no difference if her eyes were open. Sometimes, she sees better with her eyes closed.

JUST ONE GLIMPSE of Abba's face can wake a lifetime of imagination. Image-nation: we are the nation made in His own image and likeness. He fixes fallen imaginations, and the child inside of her loves it.

THE FLYING mind understands her Abbaness, Likeness, Sameness, and Oneness. From this position in faith, high and lifted up, no longer suffering from thoughts of a fallen mind, she flies high on eagle's wings mentality. She lives and moves and has her being in Love's co-seated Savior.

．　．　．

SHE WAS TRANSPORTED into faith by love alone. Thinking of this makes it easy for her to spread her wings.

THE FLIGHT IS UPWARD and inward. She taps her chest and whispers, *You are home. You came back. My body is your Throne home.*

IN FAITH, we remind others of the imagination of flight and being co-seated in Christ. When others suffer from the imagination of failure and heaviness, we remind them that the burden was lifted and removed. They are free to fly too.

GOOD NEWS! Abba has placed us in this position in faith. It's so beautiful and real that it feels too good to be true. We are trembling with the magic of flight that wants to spill out of us in every direction, uncontrolled and influencing all in grace.

FREEDOM. Believing. Wonder. Magic. Grace. Faith. Love. Flying. Paradise. Imagination.
   Likeness Redeemed. Innocence Restored.
   No separation, only Union.

16

GRACELING

Once you've tasted pure grace, you are
spoilt for life. Grace rules. The Lordship
of Jesus is established upon the dynamic
of his goodness (1 PETER 2:3).

S*it back and smile. Enjoy Our love.*
Enjoy Our union.
Feel free to giggle.
The giggles come with grace.

SHE IS all warm and stuffed with poetry and dreams.
Abba gives her a sense of perpetual happiness. She
can't stop smiling. She once admitted to icing her jaw
from all the smiling. Her smile is contagious. She grins
like the Son himself is rising inside of her.

. . .

SHE'S A GRINNING GRACELING. She knows a Graceling when she sees one. It takes One to know all. And her smile spreads.

The Gracelings grin, giggle and glow. They are glowing from knowing they are so loved. Their smiles show they know.

She glows. She can't stop glowing. She persists in glowing, and there is a soft, silvery light around her.

SHE GRINS as she reads of Claire of Assisi, *Bright, Claire*. It is said she would come from prayer with her face so shining that it would dazzle everyone around her. What a glow! The glow of great grace is evident on this Gracelings face.

SHE CONTEMPLATES grace and perceives a gleam in her heart, an infinitude of colors so vibrant and radiant and full of life. She is like a walking rainbow.

At the thought of great grace, her face became so joyful, her eyes so bright, her heart so jubilant, and all her inner senses sang a melisma: *I am full of You. I am full of You. I am full of You.*

HE HAS CROWNED her life with smiles and lots of sugar. She speaks glowingly of the way He loves her. She is soft and quick to laugh. She's giggling, grinning, and glowing.

Amazing Grace is her life; she glows because she knows what He has done!

> *Increasingly overwhelmed with grace as his*
> *divine influence within me, I become*
> *fully aware and acquainted with the*
> *awareness of our oneness (2 PETER 1:2).*

Oh, the tenderness of this grace. She's sweetly and ecstatically acquainted with the pleasure of Union. Deep in her soul, Abba speaks in giggles and grace.

JUST LET ME LOVE YOU, Grace says.

Let go and be held.

You'll be glad you did. I'll hold you in greasy grace.

You'll see. If you stay here in My grace embrace, you'll be covered in no time. Everything and everyone will be affected by My grace. You'll see.

No need to muster up a blessing for your enemies here. In grace, you'll see We are One.

No us and them, only All.

I have the grace you need way down deep in your soul. Get what you need from Me, and then just let the giggles roll.

ABBA HAS 1,000 different ways to lead her eyes to discover his immense grace. This glorious grace can only be perfectly communicated through public displays of divine affection (massive quantities of eternal PDA).

SHE HAS A VERY GRACED LIFE; you can tell by the giggles and smiles. She is filled with overflowing grace. She is aware that the Trinity really like her. She and her Beloved are intimate terms of affection. He calls her Graceling and predestined the world for enjoyment and bliss.

THE GIFT of grace speaks an entirely different language. It translates into countless deviations of acquittal and inno-cence (Francois du Toit). It is way out of proportion and the cause of great giggles. The boundless reservoir of grace is the suspect of great enjoyment.

> *Grace and peace have been branded into my*
> *life rather than reward and striving*
> *(1 CORINTHIANS 1:3).*

Grace is all that happens. Could not lovers say that every moment in their Beloved's arms was grace? (St. John of the Cross and fellow Graceling).

17

BEYOND REASON

*S*omething whole has appeared that has no beginning or end. I see the invisible, that which is bare of all form, not compiled of parts but infinite greatness. I see through participation, immeasurable, inseparable, inexhaustible. I see in my soul, pure light – this miracle of my soul, full of awe, stirs my soul and causes me to write (St. Symeon, The New Theologian, *Love Songs to God*).

YOU'VE LINGERED in the realm of logic long enough. Let go. No need to figure out faith. We go where logic and reason will not take us, beyond natural sight and into Union.

I'M STANDING on the edge of my mind. Human logic is behind me as I enter the Divine Milieu. I'm swept up in the currents of grace as I fly without activity to places I've never been before, and it's thrilling. I'm caught on the thermals of Abba's grace. I don't have to move a single feather, and I fly with no self-effort. Far from human analysis and imagination of lessness, I fly.

THE PATH of being who Abba designed me to be will look like insanity to the natural mind. Just look at Love's Only Begotten Son. *Time witnessed the death of an individual. Eternity witnessed the death and resurrection of all mankind* (Francois du Toit).

Most reality is invisible. Darling, I'll turn your dreams into realities. You can trust Me to take you where your heart longs to go beyond human reasoning and understanding. I've got you, My snow-white little lamb.

REASON CANNOT LIVE with love ravings. The madness of love has nothing to do with human logic. Love is beyond rationalism and logical thinking. Lovers aren't logicians.

EVERYONE on the edges of reasoning gets critiqued. Just giggle and enjoy Union. Fuller and deeper living lies beyond reason and on the highway of love.

There's no rhyme or reason to grace. It is unconscionable. Grace only makes perfect sense to unconditional love.

.   .   .

GENIUS SIMMERS in Abba's eyes. His agenda was our glorification, likeness redeemed, and original innocence restored so we would enjoy eternal Union. Our great Abba is a love genius.

OH, the geniusness and ginormousness of Abba's grand plan to include the entire human race in Love's eternal embrace. The attention to every detail to make this happen is beyond all reason and logic. He watched over his word to perform it.

HE CREATED A FOOLPROOF PLAN, ensured by His oath and promise, so humans could not mess it up (HEBREWS 6:13, Patrick Emery, The Mirror Word Bible Study Group, Facebook).

WE COME from a dimension where the original thought and conversation of the Trinity remains preserved and intact without contamination. And we are those thoughts! Love's plan will take you far beyond the realm of reasoning.

There is a greater reality beyond reason or what is sensible. Whatever you've heard about the kingdom within doesn't compare to the reality. It's more! It's the closest thing to magic in this world you'll ever experience.

18

THE COSMIC CHRIST

He is the initiator of all things; therefore,
everything finds its relevance and its
true pattern only in him
(COLOSSIANS 1:17).

I see you through the magic immensities of the cosmos. To live the cosmic life is to live dominated by the consciousness that one is an atom in the body of the mystical and cosmic Christ (Pierre Teilhard de Chardin).

THE WHOLE WORLD is permeated with God's energy, which flames out everywhere like electricity and lightning, yet most are unaware due to the toils of life.

Smeared with toil and seared with trade, we've lost touch with nature and consumed ourselves with work. Despite man's insensitivity, the nature of things can never be damaged because the Life of God is in all things. That's grace!

ALL OF CREATION is a revelation of God's being.

Are you aware of the richness of cosmic life and the immense abundance of living in the life of Christ on earth?

The meaning and matter of all life is a Man. He came that we might have a relationship with Life. Oh, the Union to be enjoyed in the totality of life surrounding us in each selah moment.

CHRIST'S LIFE pulsates through the universe like a blazing fire, almost too dazzling for some.

Christ is the center of every human being. The radiant heart of Christ is alive and pulsating with love in everyone (Pierre Teilhard de Chardin).

See these eight billion incarnations and expressions of Christ in so many varieties? Everyone is physically Christified.

HE IS SUPREME AND CEASELESS. He animates, without disturbing, all of Earth's processes in magnificent detail. Can you feel the beating heart of Christ in the matter of all things?

The whole world is an extension of the Trinity; the

Cosmic Christ is the Incarnate Being in the heart of all matter. The whole world is incarnate.

CAN you see a Man in every atom?

CHRIST IS the primacy in the mystery of Creation.
Christ is the Alpha and Omega.
Christ was and is human and divine.
Christ was and is cosmic.
The entire cosmos is in communion
(Pierre Teilhard de Chardin).

(EXCERPTS FROM THE COSMIC CHRIST, Pierre Teilhard de Chardin).

19

THE ADORABLE ONE

T*his is My well-pleased Son inside of My well-pleased sons. And the whole earth is filled with My Adorable glory.*

HE IS THE ADORABLE ONE, making all adorable sons.

ABBA SAYS, *I am even more beautiful in persons.*

I'LL NEVER FORGET his arms around me. There's no way he'll let you walk past him without reaching out to hug you. Freedom holds me, and I'm bound to delight in him.

. . .

THE MOST ADORABLE One is tenderhearted and mad with joy. He is the elixir of eternal life. I am filled with wonder and wild desire at the sight of his beauty.

I LOSE myself in his adoration for me. I plunge into the unfathomable and inexhaustible beauty and find peace in the Most Adorable Son. I am absorbed in this undefined immensity and consumed in the fiery transparency of limitless love. I taste, see, feel, and touch the Might, the Radiant, the Adorable Risen Son.

THE HEIGHT of his love has drawn her upwards and makes her One (Beatrice of Naz).

THESE ADORABLE EYES ARE LOVELY, lovely, lovely, like nothing I've ever seen. They're full of secrets like seafoam and prickle rich with mystery. His Adorableness is full of whispers and caresses.

IT IS ENCHANTING ENOUGH to seek you, but more enchanting to be held by you. The former is the task, and the latter is sheer joy. Oh, to embrace you is surely enchanting, for your very touch is rewarding (Gilbert of Hoyland).

. . .

THE SIGHT of his reckless beauty against the sky and wind-scrolled sea takes my breath away. As I see his loveliness, it overwhelms me. He shares his loveliness with me. Everything he is, he has shared with me. The Most Adorable One has made me adorable.

HE LIFTS MY CHIN. There's no accusation in his eyes, only love. And his love clings to me like my own skin. The loveliest of all has made me lovable. His smile sends shockwaves of love and approval through me.

LIGHT-FULL AND LOVELY IS SHE.
   Love lends fullness to beauty.
   Love and beauty, Incarnate Son
   Beauty so ancient and so lovely.
   Beautiful are the things that are seen.
   More beautiful are the things that are understood
(Henry Suso).

LOVELY, lovely, lovely, oh my soul is the loveliest of all. His adorable touch has healed whatever aches my heart. I kiss the most Adorable Face of my face with my first breath in the morning, and I fly. I am immersed in one great bliss that transcends all pleasure and pain.

He is the Adorable One who makes all adorable to me. Our lives are tailor-made for adoring and affection.

20

GOOD NEWS

No one can afford to underestimate and be
blasé about this final message; a salva-
tion of such magnificent proportions...
(HEBREWS 2:3A).

G*ood News makes me happy. It's not Good News*
if it doesn't make me happy.
   Good News depends on God. If it depends
on me, it's not Good News (Patrick Emery, The Mirror
Bible Study Group, Facebook).

SALVATION'S ECSTASY is to be experienced. The heart of
the Gospel is Christ in everyone and the nitty-gritty
essence of Oneness.

. . .

The Gospel is *universal and addressed to all because we are One* (Julian of Norwich).

The Gospel asks for nothing in return; there are no strings attached. The bliss of the Gospel is that we have been saved from doing it ourselves.

> She *finally knew that no contribution from*
>   her *side could possibly assist God in*
>   *fulfilling his promise*
> *(see Romans 4:19b).*

The Good News is that the work is all done. *It is finished* and cannot be added to or underestimated.

> *Overwhelm me with the understanding of*
>   *the magnitude of the power in the*
>   *finished work of Christ*
> *(Ephesians 1:19).*

The cross did the job. There is nothing left to fix. We were born right, and we need to know it.

That's Good News. We are licensed to live!

Work all done; sin is dealt with. Christ has rescued our minds from all unworthiness and condemnation.

He paid it all.

The Gospel is not retributive, only restorative.

. . .

INTO THE FINISHED WORKS, I go, exploring. With sin no longer on the agenda, I am free to be me and live loved. I'm no longer trying to become what I already am by his righteousness.

The Good News is we are in him to begin with. No amount of striving or self-effort can place us here. *Here* is where we have always been.

> *Of God's doing are we in Christ*
> *(I CORINTHIANS 1:30B).*

That's Good News! The Gospel is His likeness redeemed (righteousness) and innocence restored (original design) in all humanity. Our original pre-Adamic design was restored and rebooted to the original settings. To restore, one must have the Original in mind.

I SAW Three Beings standing in a Rock.
    The first One said my name, Daughter.
    The second said, It is finished.
    The third One said, Now, Let's be together.
    Then They all said, Enjoy My love.

21

PERPETUAL PERFECTION

But now we have an exception. In complete
contrast to the previous priesthood, this
priest offered a single sacrifice of
perpetual efficacy for sins. To celebrate
the perfection of what was attained
through his single sacrifice, he sat down
as the executive authority of God
(HEBREWS 10:12).

The Son's single sacrifice is forever effective. The Son of perpetual perfection is permanently unfolding my purification, which he has attained once and for all.

TRANSPORTED BY LOVE ABOVE EVERYTHING, by the sublime excess of the Spirit, I realize the perfection of all God's children.

Some people can only appreciate things if they are perfect. Others see perfection in all and appreciate it.

HE ACCOMPLISHED our perfect perpetual purification and sat down. His sacrifice is effective forever. He sat down to celebrate our perfection. His Throne endorses our likeness redeemed and innocence restored.

I AM PERPETUALLY PERFECT.

He has zero records of any imperfection. I've been scrutinized in the rays of the Son and found flawless. He has done it all. We can add nothing. Our part is to enjoy this perfection and purification of sin.

ENJOY LIFE AS A LILY. We have been perfected.

> *The temptation is to exchange the truth*
> *about our completeness with the idea of*
> *incompleteness and shame; thinking*
> *that perfection requires your toil and*
> *manner of wearisome labor*
> (2 CORINTHIANS 11:3).

We are perfect, and he has made us so.

·   ·   ·

I'M PLUNGED into the All-Inclusive One, the One so perfect that I lose myself in the ultimate perfection of my own individuality (Pierre Teilhard de Chardin).

PERPETUAL PERFECTION IS a true characteristic of love.

22

FOSSIL MAN

Look to the Rock from which you were
cut/hewn, and to the excavation of the
quarry from which you were dug
(ISAIAH 51:1B, Amplified Bible).

The Rock is the matter of all matter. Look at the science of stone. In bedrock, we find geologic truth. The secrets revealed in bedrock can tell you what happened right here, in this spot you are in, hundreds of years ago.

JUST AS BEDROCK holds the memory and history of the land. The Rock from which I am hewn has inscribed his likeness and image into the marrow of bones and DNA in innumerate detail.

I mirror his likeness in every way imaginable. My likeness has been preserved in the Rock. Although I may have forgotten, he has not (Francois du Toit).

ABBA IS MY BEDROCK. He has preserved my redeemed likeness and restored my original innocence.

WHAT IF GOD has hidden himself where no one would think to look? Inside of Hewn-man beings.

Inside of his life, he has preserved my life. I am a fossil containing and holding the evidence of all Life's life. The Life-giving life to all has made an impression in me. I hold his image.

We search for God, and here he is within us, hiding within our very DNA. Hidden under the layers of your life is the truth of what God believes about you.

MANKIND'S ORIGIN and true identity are preserved and revealed in the Rock of Ages. (In those days, the term 'rock' represented the 'hard drive' in computer language, where data is securely preserved for a long time.)

Rock fossils carry the oldest data and evidence of life, and so do we. As a fossil is preserved in the Rock, our lives are preserved in him (1 PETER 2:6, COMMENTARY, FRANCOIS DU TOIT).

23

BRIGHT PEARL PALACE

*He has taken up residence in my human
skin to be in the closest possible association of Oneness. We are inseparably
entwined (REVELATION 21:3).*

*O*nce again, I see him wholly within my house,
and amid these furnishings, he arose unexpect-
edly and united and bound himself to me in an
inexpressible, ineffable manner. He made me like fire and
light. Being united with him, how shall I tell you who he is
– this vibrating flame (Hildegard of Bingen).

OH, this mysterious and most beautiful palace of me.
Deep in my soul lives a king and a kingdom beyond
time and space. His eternal life is in me, and I am his
sweet delight.

. . .

I DREAMED of a palace filled with perfect pearls bountiful in color, from the gleam of blood-red pearls to the luster of violet velvet. Each one is personally beautiful.

The Beloved sings, and the pearls dance. He has a particular fondness for dancing pearls in the light of the Son. And the pearls love the Sundance.

LIGHT DIVINE, Son of mine, we are Your pearls. We are Your palace. Lover of my life, love diver, deep dive love. He dives deep and cuts through the working waves so that he may fetch his dearly loved pearls.

I DREAMED DEEPER STILL. I had a pearl inside my chest that shown with a brilliant light. Every light in the house is on and surely shines the Light of the World. This true light shines with bold certainty and flawlessness and illuminates my temple-palace.

THE BELOVED SON shines forth from within the pearls of the world he created. He has become visible in my windows for all to see.

My glorious Lord Christ, my Divine influence secretly diffused and active in all and all, and the dazzling center on which innumerable pearls meet.

The Light of the Bright Pearl Palace is the beating heart empowering the entire world.

. . .

ALL MY HOMES are fully furnished and lavishly decorated.

Look at these cathedrals of mystic beauty and dreamy grace. The single most beautiful place in all of creation is the human heart. It was made for him.

I am a plenteous palace, a mansion of immense beauty and higher learning.

WHAT IF WE don't study or learn the Word? What if we are born with the Word alive inside of us? What if the Word is Christ?

What if we remember that perfect love has been embroidered, plaited, and braided within our hearts?

What if we are born with a Pearl alive on the inside?

I, Rachael Suzanne Cannon (your name here _____), in the gentle ocean tide, look at the Son gazing on me and gaze into my own heart. And there I see him, more brilliant than a million noonday suns. And now I understand that I am wholly occupied by God! I find the pearl of Christ within and kiss him.

Thank you, Mon Tresor.

HE HAS SET his truth so sweetly and so deeply in my inward temple. What a lovely temple! The king opens the palace door and points out a few features but lets the rooms speak for themselves.

PLEASANT IS the theme of the Bright Pearl Palace. A plenteous and bright place indeed, where honey and cream do wondrously abound.

24

CHARMS OF LIFE

All of my relationships are impacted by my
acquaintance of love's completion in me
(PHILIPPIANS 1:9).

O ne by one, I see, and I love all those you have given to charm and adorn my love of life (Pierre Teilhard de Chardin).

THESE BEAUTIFUL CHARMS of life are my friends. I am rich. Abba has indulged me.

These darling friends of mine have made my heart a sweet scene. I've won the lottery in people. I am charmed by the faces of love in every color and language. I wish to know all and be known by all, not according to the flesh, but according to love.

. . .

WE CAN SWEETLY and authentically say, *Namaste*. Christ in me sees the Christ in you, and what a charm you are to my life.

INSIDE OF CHRIST, the world is alive and bright and full of charms. He shows me hidden angles and new perspectives, and we talk about them one by one.

He is the life of all and astral. I revel in his beauty in people.

> *We are the object of your favor and friend-*
> *ship. Well done, God! You are the Father*
> *of compassion and the God in whom*
> *everyone is equally esteemed*
> *(2 CORINTHIANS 1:2-3).*

You have given me your very charms of life for my own delight. Don't judge others; enjoy them in love.

EACH SOUL IS A CRADLE, *and the Beloved lays here. Each soul is a charming stable, warm with new life and uncondi-tional love* (Mechthild of Magdeburg).

> *This unveiling of love redefines human life*
> *(2 CORINTHIANS 5:15).*

This is the great awakening. This is a radical and

most defining metanoia moment. We are his treasures, his charms of life.

> *The indwelling love of God compels one to*
> *live sensitively aware of the people*
> *around us (1 JOHN 3:17).*

I CHERISH people as the charms of my life. My specialty is endorsing and debuting their value. We add beauty to each other's lives.

25

WHAT'S IN A NAME?

*Her love is not defined by her love for God
but by his love for her. She has always
had his undivided attention and affection, as demonstrated in His Son's work
of At-one-ment (1 JOHN 4:10).*

I have named you Made-of-Me. Now, let Me remind
you of the meaning of your name.

I smiled when I saw my Abba's face. I was
looking for a friendly place and a friendly face. I
looked in his face, and he said my name. His eyes were
glittering and misty like mine.

I FELT around inside myself for my true name, and
though it took a long and lonesome moment, I finally
felt it there. It was scintillant around the edges, and it

was mine. My name was sweet and shiny inside my chest, and I grinned.

WONDER SWEPT through my heart like a wave at the name he gave me. I felt it like a fire burning inside. I felt heat and light like a flame in my belly, alive for the first time, reminding me of who I am. I am loved for being myself and not for what I do.

MY NAME IS RACHAEL. I'm a little lamb. My name is Rachael Suzanne. I am a little lamb, a snow-white lily, a trumpeter of likeness redeemed and innocence restored.

EVERY TIME SOMEONE ADDRESSES ME, I'm reminded I am *Made-of-Me*. I glow, I grin, and I giggle.

YOUR NAME IS RACHAEL. You are Made-of-Me.
 You are My kind.
 We are in this together, he whispers to my heart.
 I am with you.
 Your name is your reminder.
 I made it so you would remember.
 Be your name.
 You are a very marvelous one;

The one whose thoughts are flooded with light.
I have adorned you in Love.
My precious, My prime investment, My inheritance,
My treasure and My trophy wife.

26

THE PATHWAY OF MARVELS

F*ollow the trail I've blazed through my death, descent, resurrection, and ascension. I've placed you here in My Father's arms.*

THIS PATH of mine is beautiful, and so is yours. Each is distinct and unique. I've taken the long way around and found all things beautiful. There is no way he has not made.

The way stretches before me, unhindered and ablaze with light. Never has it been so clear before. Never has it felt so bright.

In the beauty of this life of love are inexpressible ecstasies and wildfires. I have immortal longings in me, and the tasting room of heavenly delights is always open for indulgence. Abba made a realm called Pleasure and placed us here. I shall enjoy this Triune delight forever.

. . .

THE PLEASURES of God you experience in your quiet time are about to spill out on everyone you meet.

WHERE THE GRASS is crushed lies a fresh pathway deeper into the luscious meadow. The blades wave and bow in the wind. See me resting here beside this mirror of reflection in still waters?

My mind steps in Selah footprints. I pause to marvel, and I am raptured. I travel by way of contemplation. I ponder Love, and I am high.

THIS HIGHWAY, the pathway of marvels, is a misty-eyed path as our awareness of effortless Union and outrageous grace grows. Oh, the grace that reaches out for me and carries me away. I get distracted. There are so many things I want to look at along the way that I forget where I'm going. What if I'm already here, and all the fun is from looking, exploring, and enjoying this moment right now?

IN MY UNDERSTANDING, all my paths have led me to Abba, for he is everywhere. With omnipresence in mind, I find the freedom to go on more excursions.

27

DIVINE BEAUTY

Christ is my significance and makes me
beautiful (GALATIANS 3:28).

She walks in divine beauty, for he has made all things beautiful. The breath of divine beauty blows everywhere and she inhales.

There's nothing shallow about appreciating beauty. This world is too beautiful, and it must be adored.

SHE IS A DELICATE BEAUTY, extremely light in a way that seems too perfect for this world. Yet here she is, the prettiest, most ethereal romantic. A delicate, tender, refined, and sublime beauty.

SHE IS HEAVEN.

. . .

SHE'S a woman of extraordinary passion and sensitivity. Her deepest desire is to explore the Abba love in the essence of all things which hold us together.

SHE PROBES into the mystery of Christ in us. At the center of the cosmos is Abba's living, beating, beautiful heart with the fiery energy of love and compassion.

HER ENTIRE OUTLOOK is divinely mystical and beautiful. She has a great love for beauty. She sees all things together lovely. Her brow shines from kisses, young and healthy. Gentle, soft, and beautiful in color, she glows like a girl gilded in gold at sunset. She is the color of Union.

I BEHOLD A MOST WONDROUS BEAUTY. *Myself is glory, full of pure light, unencumbered and weightless* (Mechtild of Magdeburg).

THE BEAUTY and the beautifier are effortlessly One. I find the One in many. His beauty was planted and multiplied.

I AM EVEN MORE *beautiful in persons,* he says.

28

GOD IS MIND-FULL OF ME

*I wear a built-in helmet like a halo with
expectations of redemption realities and
salvation declarations (EPHESIANS 6:17).*

*You have freed my mind in order to redis-
cover your image and likeness in me
(1 PETER 1:19, COMMENTARY, FRANCOIS DU
TOIT).*

A mind made up is a made-up mind.
My mind was born from above.

A MIND not flying thinks thoughts of lessness.

God is mind-full of us. He overwhelms my
thoughts of lessness with moreness and reminds me
that he knew me before he formed me.

. . .

MY MIND WAS MADE in him. My mind was made in *Up*.
My mind is meant for flight.
My mind is wired for weightlessness.
Brows are for kissing. Abba's lips are tattooed in my
mind. I have the mark of sugar on my forehead.

HEAR MY VOICE, My darling.

*My words are full of love and life. There is no assump-
tion or negativity in My whispers, no hints of accusation,
condemnation, or slander; No suspicions or regret, blame or
judgment.*

*If you hear thoughts of lessness, it's not Me. Stop. Take a
deep breath. Find your co-elevated spot and listen again. I
love you. Can you hear me?*

Let the revelation of redemption shape your thoughts.

THE FLYING mind has been masterfully crafted in a
heavenly place. I have the same mind as my co-seated
Christ. I am interfacing now, even as I write. My mind
is purified from all the heaviness of sin- consciousness and raised to heavenly things, like innocence
restored.

RELAX YOUR MIND. The mind of Christ is designed to be
weightless. It's as natural as breathing. Living this God-

fused life is easy. If it's not easy, it's not the God-fused life. It's probably religion.

Living in the well-done opinion of Abba renews my mind to his unconditional love. It's his love that dispels the ministry of accusation and condemnation.

> *Now, I enjoy a delightfully different frame*
> *of mind. Because of Christ, every time I*
> *encounter weakness, I escape into the*
> *strength of my I-am-ness*
> (2 CORINTHIANS 12:10).

> *The temptation was to trade our complete-*
> *ness for incompleteness*
> (2 CORINTHIANS 11:3).

Losing altitude speaks of the mind-fall, which are thoughts and beliefs of incompleteness and lessness. The flying mind believes what God believes.

BE RENEWED in your innermost mind. Ponder the truth about you as in Christ, and begin with your co-seatedness. This will cause your re-programming. We are co-elevated, and our minds are wired for flight.

Nothing is wrong with our design. We were mind-fallen, blinded, darkened in our unbelief, and grounded in our thinking (Francois du Toit).

· · ·

NOW THAT CHRIST has rescued us from the fallen mind, we are free to rediscover our likeness redeemed and our innocence restored.

IF YOU MUST PROBE your interior life, look for Me!

If you love a good mystery, come and find Me within. I've hidden Myself here inside every detail of your life. You'll be delighted. Trust Me, I did it this way because I love you deeply and want you to know we have never been apart.

29

TOUT EST NOUVEAU

*This is the official inauguration of our new
life. A brand new way of life has been
introduced all because of his flesh torn
on the cross (HEBREWS 10:20).*

I dropped my memories into his lap as I lay my head on his heart. New life spilled out over me from his eyes.

*You are part of a new human race created
and defined in Jesus Christ at the cross
(EPHESIANS 2:15).*

*Here's the secret of my newness; Whatever
is true of Jesus is equally true of me
(see 1 JOHN 2:8).*

I'm done doing what's already been done. All that I

knew before, now seems worthless. We were rebooted into newness by our joint resurrection with Jesus, and now we share the same fellowship he enjoys with the Father and Spirit.

HIS RESURRECTION LIBERATED the atomic energy of life on a massive scale. It set in motion a chain of reactions that has made man a new being, hitherto unknown to even himself (Pierre Teilhard de Chardin).

DON'T THROW away pieces of yourself to fit into somebody's old wineskin. Be you! You are new to begin with. I've ordered your steps. I've got you, and you are Mine. You are a new creation. Steal the show and live wild, free, and oh so loved.

ONE OF THE greatest tragedies of religion is conformity. The newness of Christ gives me the freedom to be me. This is a whole new world of freedom and love. It is delightful and sweet. It becomes me!

I make all things New. The crux of the Gospel is the old way of performance-based life is over.

> *Behold, Wow! I have made all things new*
> *(REVELATION 21:5).*

30

FINGERTIPS TO CHEST

*Come to the conclusion for yourselves of his
indwelling! Should it appear to you that
Christ is absent in your life, look again;
you have obviously done the test wrong
(2 CORINTHIANS 13:5).*

I hear the whistle of love stirring in the warm
breezes of my heart, and I feel butterflies.

IN THE INNER WINE CELLAR, *I drank of my beloved. And
when I went abroad through this valley, I no longer knew
anything, and I lost the herd I had been following. There, he
gave me his breast. There, he held me and nurtured my
soul. He taught me the science of sweetness. And I gave
myself to him without reserve. There, I promised to be his
bride. I no longer tend the herd nor have any other work.*

My every act is love. Imprinted by the grace in his eyes, I lay my neck in the gentle arms of my beloved (St. John of the Cross).

I KNOW HIM HERE, and I pressed my fingertips to my chest. He has set his truth so sweetly and deeply in my inward temple. Looking at the Son, I gaze into my own heart and find him here.

I AM A WARM, wild soul,
    A sweet height of being.
    Imbued in loving-kindness,
    Profound in tenderness.
    Sweet like honey,
    And rich in friendships.

HE IS my original and final face, my revolutionary of glory, and I am the body of Love. Fully grasp the reality of the indwelling Christ, here. I tap my fingertips to my chest. He is alive in me and holding me right in here. In this place of Union, the complete treasure of all wisdom and understanding is alive in me.

HE LIFTS the veil to show that he exists in everyone. He is the root of all he planted, the light that enlightens the world (Julian of Norwich).

. . .

THE PROMISED LAND is not a geographical location. It is one new Incarnate Man that represents and embraces an entire human race (Francois du Toit).

Self-examination is not for picking yourself to pieces. It is about finding the Trinity alive inside you, complete and whole. Every part of my body beats with Christ's heartbeat. He seems to occupy all the available space, to press out into the four corners of my earth, as if he has orchestrated and designed everything to live in me.

WONDER OF WONDERS, I've been shown where God lives; indeed, it is heaven. I tap my fingertips to my chest and grin.

BEHOLD WHO IS HERE.
    Behold who is here.
    Behold who is here.

I TAP my fingertips to my chest.

31

INDELIBLE WORDS

In my understanding, I am perfectly articulate (1 CORINTHIANS 14:20).

She speaks indelible words that create a safe space for others to feel loved and valued.

She speaks a language she did not learn with her mind but knows by heart. Nothing is distorted or disfigured in her words, and there's no hollow or empty talk. Nothing can match a heart that genuinely values others. Out of her heart flows value.

SHE INDULGES in Spirit intoxication and speaks from the ecstasy of being so loved. It's inviting.

She speaks love, imperishable value, and fullness to all she meets.

Oh, sweet living words kindle in us ever sweetly Thy love (Mechtild of Magdeburg).

. . .

SHE USES HEAVENLY words to articulate this ecstatic Union. Her words are deeply fertile. You can drink of her images and grow in the wild ecstasies of love.

Her sounds and facial expressions are full of nourishing love. There is no belittling bone in her body.

SHE WRITES words that lead to the experiential love of Abba. Consider the thought of being so loved and feel the unexpected warmth kindle within your soul.

HER GAZE and her soul are not bound or ensnared to the Book. Nope, not a Book, but a Man with Love in his eyes. He is like a door opening, taking us to places where everything is alive, in vibrant color, and humming with the powerful energy of love. Everything is alive in Christ. See?

SHE WRITES of ecstatic encounters with Love that become a form of virtual reality. She writes to evoke the listening child within us all.

SHE KNOWS how to use her pen as a lightning bolt of love to awaken a heart that is longing to remember its origin in God. Remember?

· · ·

MAY the words of this book be a mirror that gives sight to the blind. May they be felt or seen miraculously, much like a kiss, or a magic trick, or the flipping of a switch. May these words precipitate a sense of transcendence, leading you, my lovely reader, to see Christ and be held by him. Feel his nail-scarred hands place you safely on high? At the heart of these words is a love experience, a Stronghold.

THESE WORDS WORK like a spiritual hot air balloon, linking you to a world on high, which is really within. This pen is a link to the love in his eyes. Read and see.

THESE INDELIBLE WORDS are special in saying the unsayable and strangely profound.

SHE WAS BORN A WORDSMITH. She writes something she would like to read. As a scribe, she writes down a lot of conversations. She talks with the grains of sand and listens to the tales of the stars. Once, she met a seashell, and it told her of world travels and how it was formed in love at the bottom of the sea.

· · ·

SHE LEARNS by looking at his beautiful face and eyes that hold no judgment. So many times, we hide behind glazed words or practiced expressions. Abba isn't like that. His expressions make his feelings obvious. She writes about the obviousness of being so loved.

She hides in him, in his love, and forgets time. It feels scarcely human to be drawn into such a deep dimension of Union. It is effortless and, oh, so free. From here, she attempts to express concepts that transcend the power of language.

LOVE HAS AWAKENED her desire to write enlightened words. Some may not be seen on the page, but they can be felt in the heart. We have an inner knowing, a deeper knowledge of agape beyond academia. Love is a language to be felt more than heard.

SHE WRITES well-marked words of Sonship, of likeness redeemed and innocence restored. Each letter is a quiver gilded with giggles and laughter. Her words aim at the heart: *You are unconditionally loved.* They drip with the internal sweetness of living water.

SHE WRITES in Union-inspired language and morsels of the closest possible proximity. Her indelible words are delicacies of In-ness.

. . .

She writes of Sonship, and her words vibrate with meaning. She sees all things in Him and writes of that.

She doesn't miss her mark. Her words are drenched in redemption and likeness. She builds houses and repairs ancient ruins with a word. She reminds the houses they are Love's home and all the lights are on.

She outlines Abba's face for her readers so that when they see his, they will see their own.

32

FEARLESSNESS

Become fully acquainted with his gift in
you; there is nothing timid about it; the
dynamic of a mind liberated in the
spirit of love is fearless and unstoppable
(2 TIMOTHY 1:7).

I met Abba's gaze and held it, drawing from his fearless love. He has carried me away far beyond the reach of all harm.

WHERE THERE IS CONTROL, there is fear and slavery. I will not stay where I am afraid. I won't stay where I am not free.

LOVE MUST BE ALLOWED to grow wild. His love is soothing my heart and calming my fears. I'm enjoying the moment now, not living in the future. Fear is not a force in itself; it is merely the unawareness of love. Fear and self-effort are best friends.

I DIDN'T BRING you here to watch your life go by. I brought you here to live. I want you to be sure of My love.

In the certainty of My unconditional love, trade your expectations for sheer enjoyment.

So, how should one behave who has been raised from the dead? How should one live whose enemies have all been conquered?

I no longer look for enemies in the shadows. I stopped doing spiritual warfare. I stopped looking for demons behind every bush. Spiritual warfare was a lot like chasing butterflies. Now, I am footloose and fancy-free, knowing *It is finished* and all is well.

> *Jesus would often contemplate the fact that the entire industry of condemnation, accusation, and war was defeated in the downfall of Satan and that anyone who discovers their redeemed identity will witness the results (LUKE 10:18).*

Is anybody believing that the war has been won? Are we shadowboxing principalities that have been dealt with long ago? *There's a lot of talk about other gods and demons; they seem to be empowered by others' belief in them* (Francois du Toit).

The shadow of war that most have forgotten has already been won, still looms over some. I see its pall on their faces, sometimes constant and sometimes hidden.

BUT I LAUGH HEARTILY at the devil's defeat. I laughed even more when I saw that all is joy and *It is finished*. I've found Christ high and lifted up, and over all. I found myself there in him. And this was cause for great delight and enjoyment, and endless celebration.

NOTHING TO FEAR, for God dwells in me, and I in him. And he is all goodness and sweetness. I only recognize and identify fear because it seems so less a part of me that it doesn't belong to me.

I HAVE ALWAYS BEEN LOCKED into Abba, never once been separated. He is my stronghold, my fortress, and my safe place. He wants me. He is my strong tower and the tower that keeps everyone away who isn't contributing perfect love and healing to my life right now.

. . .

B*E GENTLE WITH YOURSELF*, *My Darling. Be patient, as you must always be patient with new pale seeds buried in dark ground. When you are stronger, you can begin to think again. But now is your time to feel and heal.*

I'm holding you in My arms, so full of love. You are safe here, held and nourished by the look of tender love in My eyes. Let My love settle you.

W*HERE THERE WERE SHACKLES*, now there are wings. There's a euphoric unspooling in my mind as love sets me free to fly, unafraid.

Self-consciousness dissolves in my awareness of Oneness. Separation anxiety causes fear. In the realm of love, the awareness of eternal togetherness and seamless union expels fear.

> *This perfect love union expels fear. Fear holds onto the expectation of crisis and judgment (which brings separation) and interprets it as due punishment. It echoes torment and only registers in someone who does not yet realize the completeness of their love union* (I J*OHN* 4:18).

N*OW*, I've developed quite a talent for laughing and living. I live in his laughter. If I must prepare for the future, I prepare for laughing and cuddling. I see myself laughing eternally. When I dream ahead, I see myself laughing. It's not circumstantial; it's *Lovestantial*.

Laughter promotes breath, and breath is life. I laugh, and my soul feels lighter and lighter.

33

POETRY OF ZOE

We are not complaining about our bodies,
even though we are often aware of our
frailties; instead, we yearn to be over-
whelmed with life. We know that every
evidence of death, even in our bodies,
will dissolve into life
(2 CORINTHIANS 5:4).

C hrist overwhelms me with Zoe-life. I know
that every evidence of death in my body will
dissolve into life.

HOW WOULD you live if you knew you would never die?

I AM QUITE ALIVE. I tend to see everything around me
as alive. I have a fresh upward focus, and my thoughts

are engaged in an eternal reality. I'm really living. New life surges through me. Everything is alive, and all things are new.

I AM LIVING in the full benefit of life: the advantage of life, the profit of life, the gain of life, the accumulation of life, and the gift of life.

I have a zest for living that's thrilling. Abba feeds my zest, and he is the ardor of my life. He loved me to life. My skin glows with life and adventures not yet had!

ONCE I WAS aware I was alive, I realized my unawareness of *Christ's-zoe-life* was blindness and life-less (less than life). I am alive. Alive, alive, alive, and glowing into a brighter existence. I have been raised into the newness of life. I'm experiencing a much fuller life now that I am living loved.

MY LORD, You are the entity, the totality of my life. You are the life-giving life to all (Teresa of Avila).

THE ECSTASY of being loved heals and grows you. This Triune love is a catalyst for the fullness of human life.

His love is the broth of life we drink.

We drink and we live.

34

LINGER OF LIFE

I t's been over a year now since the top popped off the wooden box of the four-walled coffin I was caged in. The religious elders *released* me.

I was set free to explore, and to my surprise, I have found God everywhere and in everyone.

I LOOKED where they told me not to. I read what they banned. I listened to who they threw under their religious bus. And I found who they were looking for but could not see right in front of them.

OUT OF THE RAT RACE, I began to linger.

They called to ask, *What are you doing for the Lord?*

Nothing, I replied. I grinned when I said it. It was true. I didn't have to try to be important anymore. That was altogether lovely. I cried happy tears, knowing I was free from their religious games.

I'M TAKING lots of long walks and counting petals on the flowers.

The flowers say *Abba loves me.*

That church said *What are you doing to be loved?*

The long way around is more beautiful, and there's less traffic. I like the back roads and fresh air and sugary seashores.

I AVOID the crowd to share a whisper with the waves or a birdsong. I've slowed way down and decided to enjoy being so loved. It saved my life. No, this is real life, the poetry of Zoe-life.

I FOUND a ring of Selah flowers. I paused to smell their fragrance and listen to the *Love Me's.* I've been here for a while. I can't go back to the building.

I'VE FOUND the love I've always wanted. In the Selah moments, I found Abba here (I tap my fingertips to my chest). And, I found Abba here (I stretch my arms out wide).

.   .   .

HE IS SO sweet and light, unlike the prickle of performance I felt in the coffin of religion.

YOU KNOW I'm such a fool for you.
  I'm in so deep.
  You've got me wrapped around your finger.
  Oh, I think the world of you.
  Do you have to let it linger? (Linger, The Cranberries*).*

I'VE DECIDED to enjoy long periods of leisure in which to mature in this Triune love affair. I delight in the abundant, beautiful, and extraordinary realities of creation. I see the message in the risen sun – the new day never fails to arise over an all-included earth, extending Love's embrace in rays and beams of warmth and light.

EVEN IN THE OLD COVENANT, Joshua, son of Nun, lingered after Moses (the *law)* left the sanctuary. A picture of our beloved Yeshua lingering in the skin tent he knew would be us one day. Yeshua refuses to leave the tent of meeting. We are his permanent dwelling place, always have been, and always will be. He's lingered all our lives.

. . .

HE IS HERE (taps fingertips to chest) lingering. I pause for a moment to ponder his indwelling in all of humanity.

In my mind, I linger on the faces of loved ones until I see my Beloved's face. Oh, this lingering shall be my life.

35

LITTLE PETUNIA

You greatly endear me and highly favor me
in Christ. I am intensely special to you.
Your love for Jesus is your love for me
(EPHESIANS 1:6).

The Father is very fond of me. He highly favors me. I am his favorite and the one whom Jesus loves.

MY SWEETNESS, My sweetheart, My darling, My I-am-ness, Mon Prefere, Ya Habibi. You are Made-of-Me.

You are My Godkind, My image, and very likeness.

I have shared My life with you; My righteousness, faith, grace, love, and all.

Everything I am, you are.

*You are My treasure and My delight. I created you for
My love and My enjoyment.*

I enjoy loving you. I delight in you.

You are My smile. You are My dream.

You are what the Gospel is all about.

I want you.

*My greatest desire is that you know I love you. Let Me
hold you and love on you.*

Let's spend all our days together.

I AM adorned with a love burning and fueling my soul.
I see Abba, which changes the way I see everything
and everyone.

I am intensely aware of Your presence, my lovely
Lord. I know your love, and it is extraordinary.

ABBA'S ENDEARMENT IS ETERNAL. It has always been. It
is continuous and endless. I've never not been his
darling daughter. I've never not been his favorite.

UNBREAKABLE ARE the bounds and bonds of his love.
It's intense, not based on our behavior or our reci-
procity. These terms of endearment are a relief. I'm no
longer yearning to be loved or wanting more. I'm
simply enjoying being so loved and endeared. I delve
into the intensities of being Abba's favorite.

I'm not looking for the next anymore. I am living in

the now, being so loved out of my mind, and enjoying the heaven out of it! I've discovered the greatest gift of all time. Christ is in me, and he really likes living here.

IF YOU MUST BELIEVE anything about yourself, believe you are so loved. I want you, even if no one else does or ever will;

I always have, and I always will.

My will for you is only that you know My love.

I am love and favor and charm and sweetness.

All My existence is love, and even now, I uphold you with My love. I greatly endear you. The details of your heart and mind matter to Me.

I care about you because I love you! Feel it sink in yet?

I cherish you.

Come, let's sit together in the deepest place of My love, little Petunia.

Your company suits Me.

36

CUP OF SON

*Whoever drinks from the source of this
water that I shall give will never thirst
again; because the water that I give
becomes an artesian well bursting
from within, defining the life of
the ages*
(JOHN 4:14).

S he turned to the Son and drank life from the
source of all life. One Son has made all sons.
She feels a love so relentless and divine
bursting from within her like it's been there all along.
No words to capture the wonder that rivers through
her veins and leaves her weightless.

So weightless that she drops everything.

LIFE GUSHES within until her chest feels full, and light

pours out of her eyes and mouth. The Light that is Life, in all of its fullness, has awakened.

Christ's golden life-light lights her up, and he revels in who he knows her to be. Standing here in the light, Sonlight inches across her hair, hands, and heart, warming her as if she were being hugged. She feels loved and known. She sees herself for the first time.

ALL SENSE of time drifted away, here, held in love so ebullient. There is so much more to consider than fear and failure. It's as if the completeness of being so loved has drowned her fears.

She's baptized in light, love, and life. Her body is a candle. Her hair is like a flaming wick. She's alight with love and life.

CHRIST IS the light shining through her. People see Love's face looking out through her eyes. Christ is a bottomless spring, and he feeds us. His clarity is never darkened, and we know that every light has come from him.

She is not responsible for maintaining the light in herself. All the pressure is off. Christ is the light within, and he never stops shining. Surely shines the Son!

SHE HOLDS the Son in her hands and drinks face to face. She grins and feels a bubble in her belly. Just looking at him makes her happy. She stares at the perfection and beauty of his face and sees her own flawless beauty.

In his light, the shape of her heart changes, and she glows.

ALL THINGS FLARE BRIGHTER *at My touch, pure and luminous. And I have touched all things!*

When Christ said this, more of him began to iridesce, and still more of his brightness grew till he was all over tremulant with shine and transfigured.

The Light lit up the world with his glorious presence, and the world is enlightened. The cup of the Son has made us all shining sons.

THIS GLOWING LIGHT BECOMES HER. She is shekinah, and all luminesce, surrounded by light and visible glory, glistening and shining light that is alive and longs to be seen.

It's as if she drank the Risen Son, and she shone.

37

THE BRIDE

*I will betroth you to Me forever; I will
betroth you to Me in righteousness and
in justice, in steadfast love, and in
mercy (HOSEA 2:19, ESV, English Standard Version).*

She is radiant with immortality and immaculate innocence. She is an anchoress, encapsulated in agape and insulated in Oneness.

She spends time with her Husband. She has a gardener's instinct and a carpenter's knack for building, and she can spot a rare gemstone.

SHE'S like a pinch of spark, and a hint of love, fiery and furious. She whistles while she works. There is a whistle in all she makes.

Sometimes, when she smiles, you can see her

secret strength. She leans on her Beloved. That's her secret.

She leaves a mark on everyone she meets. She walks, unaware of her own increasing beauty. Her beauty fills like water, the four corners of the earth.

CHRIST CAME with his rapture of wild love and made her his home. She lays down in pastures of unicorns and sings songs. Her heart sings songs she's always known, and now she remembers who taught them to her. Papa!

SHE SEES WITHOUT JUDGMENT.

She lives without regret.

She loves without limits.

She lives with no expectations except that she is loved by her Husband. He kisses her with the luscious lips of life. He still has a mud mustache.

SHE WALKS IN THE MAGICAL, luminescent, green waters of the Emerald Coast and feeds on Throne room rainbows.

I cherish you. She hears the waves whisper as they roll.

. . .

SHE CARRIES a private smile in her eyes. Gentleness and tenderness are the fabric of her makeup. She remembered how to nurture, and she forgot how to hate and be mean.

My Husband, she whispered, and she shone. She put her hand across her mouth, but a muffled giggle still flew out, and a sudden, sunny smile spilled across her face.

HER LIFE HAS SUPERNATURAL OVERTONES, and she is full of wonder. She's high under the influence of grace, and she lives as though every day is the first day of her life.

She is a woman of privilege and very well-kept. She gets lost in her darlingness. She knows she's precious to her Husband.

SHE IS a drop of wine from the Vine of Eden's vineyards, like a ruby frozen in time.

SHE SEES WHAT CHRIST SEES.
She counts her chicks before they hatch.
She finds coins in fish's mouths.
She eats free lunches.
She sees the flower in the bulb.
She has traveled in realms of gold.
Material wealth doesn't mean much to her.
She finds value in people.

Her Husband is her inheritance. She is a wealthy woman.

HER EYES ARE wild with love and imagination. She feasts on honey and manna. She sits beside milky streams and honey waterfalls.

SHE CONSPIRES with Christ to bless the fruit of the Vine. She's different, like she went somewhere and is full of something that can only be felt. There is more to her than can be seen with natural eyes.

OH, the ramifications of this mystical union!

SHE SPENDS time courting Christ and kindling love. The homage of courtly love overflows in a sense of wonder that God has chosen her for his lovely Son.

She fills her heart with image upon image of taste, scent, and radiance as the bride and groom mirror each other's qualities. Embracing, caressing, and growing together as they love.

I TELL you truly that every moment,
*   My Love is taking delight in me.*
*   If ever two were one, then surely we.*

O joys, infinite sweetness.
Look, shoots of glory bloom and buds in my soul.
Oh, Husband, my Love, whether I look through
my physical organs or my mental sight,
always it is you, I see (Hildegard of Bingen).

THE BRIDE IS the redeemed society of mankind
(Francois du Toit).

38

EXTRAVAGANT EXTENT OF AGAPE

*My God shall abundantly fill every nook
and cranny to overflowing in all areas
of your lives. The wealth of his dream
come true in Christ Jesus measures his
generosity towards you*
(PHILIPPIANS 4:19).

Look how obviously God is loving the world. We began in the bosom of agape. We are a bosom-begotten world and born from above in love.

The world was expecting a violent kingdom takeover, not a Man filled with other-centered love. They expected judgment, but Jesus came to love.

OUR GREAT, *great Abba is filling every nook and cranny*

with his love (Jewel Marvel, The Mirror Word Bible Study Group, Facebook).

EVERY TIME I think about the agape of God, I leave the ground. All human reasoning and logic fades in the light of his great love. The law of perfect agape has no codes or doctrine, only love. Rich are the reservoirs of Union in agape.

I SPEND my days contemplating this Man who awakened love in me to the point of breaking every other bond in my life that was not bound to true love.

Knowing him has become my obsession. The tangle of love and grace holds me inside, or I'd fall apart. I've never met a love so present in every moment and giving us his undivided attention.

He sees more of me than anyone else ever has. He holds me like I am something precious. He draws me close to find what's right, not wrong.

I WAS MADE FOR LOVING. I see God, the room around me fades, and I am aware of the fullness of Triune love. I am embosomed in his love, his pleasure, and his treasure. I feel God within myself.

.   .   .

TAKE the ride of your life on the roller coaster of unconditional love. Enjoy this blanketing love that covers unkindness.

Enjoy My love.

Helping you is My pleasure.

Enjoy all the goodies of being so loved.

39

LUMINOUS EFFLUVIA

I pray that your thoughts will be flooded
with light and inspired insight and that
you will clearly picture his intent in
identifying you in him so that you may
know how precious you are to him
(EPHESIANS 1:18A).

S ome ecstatics are known for their luminescent
radiance and brighten entire rooms with rays
of light from their bodies.

An early Christian mystic named St. John van
Ruysbroeck, known as the *Admirable*, shone with a
divine light.

IT WAS SAID that the grace of God shone in his
countenance and that none left his presence uncon-

soled. He liked to pray in the depths of the forest, where he would be rapt in ecstasy.

One day, the prayer time lasted longer than usual. His fellow contemplatives went to find him and saw a tree bathed in light in the distance. When they got near, they saw the tree surrounded by fire as John was seated and seemed intoxicated by divine love.

I HAVE RECEIVED *the ray touched by the sublime, which knows no human measure* (The Admirable).

TANGIBLE SPARKS of fire flare from some mystics as they experience the Light of Life, which spreads from the center of their souls to the body.

OH, flame of love, so living. The deepest caverns of my soul grow bright. What peace with love enwreathing you conjure to my breast, which only you, your dwelling place, may call. Wherewith delicious breathings in glory, grace, and rest, so daintily in love, you make me fall (St. John of the Cross).

IT IS SAID of Clare of Assisi that she would come from prayer with her face so shining that it would dazzle everyone around her.

The light of Christ shines out of every human face, and some gleam as if they've been fed holy honey.

THE FLOWING *fire of the Godhead has found my dry soul* (Mechtild of Magdeburg).

I AM SO DEEPLY ENTWINED *I sparkle and shine. Behold this mysterious brightness in which one sees everything* (Teresa of Avila).

THE DELIGHTFUL EFFECT *and interior sweetness of this flame of love within my soul. So sweet the devotion this love fire kindles. My soul is aglow as if a real fire burns there. If we put our finger near a fire, we feel the heat. If we near ourselves to the fire of one in love, we feel genuine warmth* (Richard Rolle).

IT IS SAID that the woman at the well (JOHN 4) emitted light after she met Jesus. Named by early church historians, *St. Photini, The Enlightened One*, she had an undeniable glow.

STEPHEN, the first martyr (ACTS 6), glowed as he was being stoned by his accusers.

· · ·

JESUS'S FACE shone like the sun on the Mount of Transfiguration, and his clothes became white as light (MATTHEW 17).

THIS BEAUTIFUL FLOODING of light pours forth inside our souls, illuminating our paths and lighting our steps. We glow because we know what God believes about humanity.

ONCE A SOUL EXPERIENCES the eternal delight of love, there remains a sort of glow and sweetness. Love is scintillant and ebullient.

Ask the fluorescent Carmelite nuns and brilliant Beguines of their Beloved and behold the luster of love.

IT'S BEEN TOLD these flames of love so surprised Maria Magdelena de Pazzi that her face became full and glowing. Her eyes shone like shining stars. She moved about in a wonderous manner. She was seen running from place to place, calling in a loud voice,

Love, Love, Love, Love, Love,

My Jesus is nothing but Love. He is mad with love. You are altogether merry and lovely.

You refresh and console. You nourish and unite.

You are effort and rest, Death and Life in One.

What is not in you?
You are wise and willful, sublime
and immeasurable, wonderful, and inexpressible
(Maria Magdalena De Pazzi).

40

SECRET TOKENS OF LOVE

So great was the feeling I had in that sweet
union that it's not to be wondered if I
was out of my senses
(St. Paul, 2 CORINTHIANS 5:13).

There is no deeper revelation than Christ in me.
That's next-level revelation (Keisha Holder,
The Mirror Word Bible Study Group,
Facebook).

The mystic life is interactive with God, interfacing
with the Trinity. It's full of intimacy, supernatural
power, and experiencing Union with God.

THIS UNION IS by grace alone. The spiritual jumping
jacks are over. No formulas are needed to get more of
God when you already have all of him in you.

. . .

How can I express what my soul has received and write it in a book? Each time I begin to write of love, I feel as though Christ sips from my cup. In his sipping, I am inebriated within.

These secret sips of delight have become my secret tokens of love. One simple thought of his smile, and I am raptured in love. A drip, a drizzle, a drink, a secret sip of divine Union. Oh, this union shall be my life.

The point of Union is love. The point of love is Union. I overflow with inner joy at the very thought of the warmth of his love. I'm so dear to Love.

Abba is lovely to embrace and so tender for the loving soul to kiss that all hearts should be fit to break with longing for Thee.

One tiny drop of union and all the joys and pleasures of this world seem small. I am swept away into the Good. How completely I have been captivated. How I have been deeply soul-touched at the sweet words of my Beloved. Your bright eyes, they shine on me (Henry Suso).

Oh, sweet love, I am never diminished in your sight, only exaggerated. I consider Abba's greatness in me and drink a secret token of love again. I am Thy throne of delight.

. . .

HE ABIDES WITH ME SECRETLY, at the table, in bed, and in the streets. I tap my fingertips to my chest and whisper, *I love you, my love.* And I am blissed with strong drink.

OH, wonder of wonders, how can it be?

You have given me a drink and have adorned me with life! Drinks are the secret tokens of love. He is more ravishing than anyone can express.

OH, you living drink, you sweet swirl,
My beautiful daughter from My Fatherly heart.
I enjoy thy beautiful bliss.
Love, Abba

41

WARM EYES

Knowing the warmth in his eyes has set me
free (1 JOHN 3:22).

Christ's eyes promise gentleness, and are full of assurance and wonder. His eyes never lose their calm. I can feel the power of love in his look. There are a hundred secrets in how he looks at me and a hundred stories.

HE GAZED AT ME, and I breathed deeper. He gave me a little wink. The trees swayed and breathed around us, though I hadn't noticed any wind or trees before. Nothing else mattered in this private look. I'm invited with a look into another world, a world of light and love and life.

. . .

I STAND in a dream of life. It's so lovely, this warm cascade of life-light coming from his eyes, that I want to slip outside my body, becoming an indistinguishable part of all Life. He has his face turned to me, and I dissolve into light.

I FELT the light transform my bones and fill my mind until I had no room for thoughts. It pooled in my eyes until I could see nothing but that gentle, dazzling stream of Golden Son flowing from his eyes. My heart spoke one last word, an astonished, expanding, *Whoaaa*, before it burst into light.

IN THE LIGHT, I see the Union of all things. In God's mind, we are in Christ.

Jesus is what God believes about us (Francois du Toit).

I see him everywhere and in everyone. Awake and alive in his eyes, I see the possibility of a different life.

FLAMES BLOOM IN HIS EYES. His eyes have a language all their own. His eyes speak. Liquid love shines from his eyes like lava; his touch is an all-consuming fire. I'm a Lady of the Fiery Eyes, burning bright from the flames of love in which we are One.

How warm is the fire in his eyes? It's like a sunbeam has awakened the world at first light. He has split the dark loneliness in my heart. The spectrum of warmth and penetrating light in His eyes leaves me marvelously enriched.

Look at the fiery, fascinating life in his eyes. His divine eyes reveal the superabundance of triumphant love.

There's a smile in his eyes when he looks at me. He beams rays of fullness at me and reminds me I am full to the brim of God.

His eyes blaze so bright I find it hard to look away. His constant presence gives me strength.

His eyes know every detail of all created things. His eyes follow the wings of swallows, and he sets his affection on the world he created.

Where I see a threat, his eyes smile. *Peace, peace.*

The eyes of my Beloved shine more brightly than the stars because in my Beloved's eyes is the sheen of understanding and love so inclusive it illuminates the world with Belovedness.

I see the beauty and power in his eyes, captivating and swift. His vibrant love and life touched me to the core of my being, and a resounding, familiar happiness filled me.

HERE, face to face, beholding your beautiful eyes, I see something I've always longed for, to be known and cherished just for me. Quirks or no quirks, only loved. Loved not for behavior but for being created. I feel that kind of love in the Beloved eyes of my Jesus.

I SEE YOU, My Darling, and I love you.
    The moment I heard his words aloud, the tension deep inside me for all these years unraveled. A lightness swept through me, and I felt a rush of freedom. I hadn't realized the weight of my own burden until now, when it lifted.

AND I LEARN BY LOOKING. His eyes give away so much. His eyes are brimming with sweetness for me. His love has found me.

LATER, I saw the same eyes in the inmates of every county jail and prison I visited. And I understood that the heart of God is at the heart of everyone.

42

OH THE BLISS

*I am blissfully out of my mind with plea-
sure in you, my Maker; he delights in
our ecstasy. Our insane mode is
between us and God; we promise to
behave ourselves sane and sober before
you (2 CORINTHIANS 5:13).*

I gaze, and I am love drunk.
   He is pouring his wine eternally.
   His name, Jesus, is nectar to be sipped.
He is the pulse of my life.
I no longer have an interest in mundane things.
*I have held the Uncreated One, and it undid me
completely.*
It opened me up so wide that all else is restrictive.
Some may know this place well, Others are coming;
All will join us (Hadewijch of Antwerp).

. . .

OH, the depths of this blissidness. I'm participating in the enormousness of bliss and Oneness that Christ suffered so dearly for me to enjoy. The overwhelming suffering our Beloved experienced brought about an equally overwhelming love and sense of inseparable Oneness.

I'm immersed in one great bliss that transcends all pleasure and pain. He is the only Adorable One to me. I have none other.

IN UNION, I became so sweetly attentive to the goodness of my well-beloved that my attention seems to be not attention but adoration and awareness that Christ is in all and is all. The beauty and bliss of life is exploring and finding love in every nook and cranny of human life and the world (St. Francis de Sales).

ME, Lord?

Callest me Thy joy, Thy love, Thy bliss.

Me, Lord?

Of these love glances, those life-kindling eyes.

Me, Lord? Us, Lord?

The center of your embrace.

Such wondrous love amazes me and leaves me blissed.

. . .

I ENJOY the unending bliss of being a family member. Love is our Father. He is the Firstling of bliss, and we are his offspring. His excess love joined us, and all are equally close. There are no runts in the litter. The Father has kissed open our eyes.

IN THE CHORDS of his bosom, I am alive. Precious balm drips from Thy hand. Its hidden power affects my soul.

His joy startled me. How joyous and welcoming his voice.

Oh, blissful love. Oh, tenderly beloved.

And now I say, Oh glorious night,

Even in night, there is light.

For there is no darkness in him

(St. Francis de Sales).

OH, the bliss of knowing that nothing has ever separated us. The bliss of gratitude and the pleasure of eternal certainty have entered my soul for good. This eternal certainty brings me such immense bliss that I am out of my mind. In this blissed assurance of effortless Union, I am anchored without fear of separation. This feeling is such a relief that I melt into peace, and it's easy to rest as though nothing on earth could hurt me.

In this place of joy, you are beyond the reach of any harm (I PETER I:9).

Our entanglement is so glorious. I am blissfully aware of our Oneness.

I HAVE FOUND myself so beautifully and completely in him. The bliss of enjoying Union has brought about my most authentic existence. Oh, this love, it is grand and magnanimous, and abounding in rich bliss.

I SHALL SAVOR with heightened consciousness the intense yet tranquil rapture of a vision whose coherence and harmonies I can never exhaust (Pierre Teilhard de Chardin).

Blessed Assurance, Jesus is mine!
Oh, what a foretaste of glory divine!
Heir of salvation, purchase of God
Born of his Spirit, washed in his blood.

This is my story, this is my song
Praising my Savior, all the day long
This is my story, this is my song
Praising my Savior, all the day long

Perfect submission, perfect delight
Visions of rapture now burst on my sight
Angels descending, bring from above
Echoes of mercy, whispers of love

This is my story, this is my song
Praising my Savior, all the day long
This is my story, this is my song
Praising my Savior, all the day long
(Blessed Assurance, *Phoebe Knapp).*

43

BARDS AND TROUBADOURS

She is a poem, and her life is full of poetry
(PHILIPPIANS 2:14).

M asters of tremulant words and iridescent singers of the Inside Seat, the verbal artists are returning ecstatic in love.

Wild poets of ecstasy and bards of blissful verse fill the golden pot of the earth at the end of the rainbow of love.

The rhyming wonderlings write musings of the land of likeness redeemed and innocence restored, filled with the wonder of it all.

Knowing the warmth in her gentle Shep-
herd's eyes inspires poetic freedom in
her every expression (I JOHN 3:22).

POETRY IS the path on the rainbow by which the soul expresses our friendship with the Son of Man. Her words are life and light, and the Oneness of God and all mankind is the theme of her melisma.

Can you hear creation singing of Oneness and the inclusion of all mankind in Christ? We sing of love in every way imaginable.

SHE WRITES of the celebration of life. She writes testimonial and experiential theology. She's all warm and stuffed with poetry and musings on love. She brings people together and sets them free in imagination to open dimensions of endless love. Her words are powerful in lovingkindness and belonging.

WORDS ARE LIVING BEINGS. She kisses them and sets them free to envelop her readers in love's embrace. She writes to nurture and nourish unconditional love, and her lines become lullabies. There's a hug in every word.

She writes in blessings and benedictions, the language of prayers, and incense rises off the pages. Her language calls to mind images of likeness redeemed, innocence restored, and the ecstasy of Union.

. . .

POET MEANS MAKER. Can you see the words come alive? She doesn't write to convey information, but to relay the ecstasy of being so loved.

Since her words are born from above, how do they work on the ground? Do they lift you up? Do they remind you of your own aboveness? Do they take you beyond sight and into I-am-ness?

SHE MAKES READERS THINK, and thinkers read. She finds new ways to express surprisingly deep truths hidden in plain sight.

UNION IS LIFE, and her word flow is Triune Voiced. *Tell them they are full of God*, she hears, and her pleromic pen moves to his voice.

> *Remember our intimate romance. The*
> *poetry of this union is the driving force*
> *of my heart (*REVELATION *2:5).*

She must write of the poetry of Almighty Love.

WHITE SAND, *warm hands,*
  Finding day, Deep day.
  Abba smiles carry me,
  Up Way.
  Born here, free hear!

All Clear, All here!
One Son, made all sons,
Hear love, Here love.
Love songs sing.
Day born nation.
Resurrection Day, Son Day.
One new Hewn-man Race.

44

LIGHT

His life is the light that defines our lives. (In his life, mankind discovers the light of life.) (JOHN 1:4).

A shard of light flashed through my mind, and my ears rang with his words, *I love you*.

The first thing I remembered was being loved and then how They nurtured me. I forgot how to hate and be mean. Loving and being loved is my nature. Hating and being mean was a learned behavior.

IN THE LIGHT OF DAY, I bloom, and something wrenched from my chest like a weight I had been carrying for a long time. My body lightened so that my tip toes barely touched the ground. Heat flashed up my arms, deep from the pit in my stomach. I looked down, and the light was pouring from my soul, a bright, white, innocent light that seemed to be dissolving all hints of separation.

When thinking fell away, I discovered a new kind of knowing. The light plunged me into the mystery of everything and lifted me up over everything.

THE LIGHT ENVELOPED MY BODY, wrapping itself in and through me until I began to glow. I am fire. I am light. In the light, I found myself quite transformed! Ah ha ha!

Oh, the eternal brightness of God, the boundless and unencompassed *Light of the World* is aglow within us all. How can we not see? The world is alive with light.

I SEE INCOMPARABLY GREATER things in the light of his face. I see how infinitely he adores us and dwells inside each temple body. He has sheathed us in his luminous warmth. I have found a tenderness and an opulent warmth in the light. It's life, and it's personal.

I AM one with the Light. The light becomes me. I run burning and shining, swelling and overflowing, too large for my skin. Uh oh, I have no skin. I am only light.

45

HEART OF MY HEART

She is innocent and childlike. She knows she
owns God's kingdom instinctively
(SEE LUKE 18:16).

She lives in childlike trust and receives the
blessing of the kingdom as effortlessly as
breathing (SEE LUKE 18:17).

The story of my heart begins in another realm. I remember God's hands bloody with my birth. My heart remembers being held. I remember the Triune hands holding me in wonder. *Look what We have made.* They marveled over me.

MY HEART IS full of his heart. And although I am now a Jubilant, I will always be young at heart. Has becoming a Jubilant made me younger, I wonder?

Beside still waters, heart of my own heart, I rest easy in love and full of wonder. Now that I know what Abba believes about me, my heart endorses my innocence.

I'VE FOUND the hart's path beside still waters, and I drink for the delight of drinking, not need (PSALM 42). This panting hart is forever satiated. Here, in my heart, lives the dearest freshness of deep down things.

> *He knows how our hearts love to reason, so he takes a little child and says, To see the significance of life hiding in a little one is to see what my Father sees in everyone. Your greatness is not how famous you can be in your own, or someone else's estimate but in discovering your individual value in your Father's embrace (LUKE 9:48).*

I have been in his arms. I have been like a child, and my heart is filled with pleasure. Whisper by wordless whisper, he soothed my lacerated heart. He hides me from those who would delight in condemning me. He restored the vitality of my heart with original likeness and innocence redeemed.

I blamed a lot on the devil, but the greatest enemy of my heart was my own inferior thinking and thoughts of lessness.

. . .

I KISS him with the lips of my heart. He is the richest Redeemer, the eternal Defender who enriches and glorifies us. Fully, richly, purely, and sincerely, his love is immense and immeasurable.

Oh my heart, what do you seek? Love.
What do these Three whisper to each other? Love.

LOVE IS the subject of Their every instinct and inmost thoughts towards us.

OUTSIDE IS FLORIDA. Inside my heart is a Paradise meadow. Oh, lovely heart, no need for panting. You have been forever satiated.

The deeper I descend into myself, the more I find Abba at the heart of my being. Hallowed life and holiness are woven through every fiber of my being.

Oh, my plentifully pleromic and childish heart! Within you is a kingdom built wholly on love.

46

ME, MINE

*I will continue to speak well of you. I will
confirm my intention always only to
bless you and to multiply you beyond
measure (HEBREWS 6:14).*

P apa, tell me a story with me in it and make me
beautiful. So he told me a story about the One
he sent to save all.

. . .

OH, sweet child of Mine. Mine, Mine, all Mine.

*It is bliss for Me to do you good. I will do for you all that
is possible to do for a creature. I will bestow on you all that
is only good.*

*I cover you in your pain because I love you. Your heart
health matters to Me. I will never scold you for being afraid
or feeling less than what I know to be true about you.*

. . .

IT'S all smiles with Papa. Purpose shines from his face. He has strong feelings of excitement for my life. His mind is made up about me.

HE'S GOT the best news I've ever heard! He's got no lessons to teach me! He's just here to experience my life through me and our unique relationship (Tehilla Luttig, The Mirror Study Bible Group, Facebook, and Founder of *The Couples Connection*).

NESTLED UNDER HIS WING, I am safe. Not even gossip can reach me here. He kisses me on the top of the head every chance he gets.

WORDS MEAN MUCH. I can live on a hearty well-done word from my Father for weeks, siphoning the fatty bits of it like a camel drawing food from its hump. It's funny how well done describes the temperature of cooked meat. I love meaty words. Well done, not medium rare. His grace-filled words fill me.

I WON'T STOP CALLING you Beloved.
   You are the daughter I've always wanted and the light of My days. You are Mine, all Mine.
   Darling, I'll take such good care of you.
   I'll reward you according to My finished work.

. . .

HE HOLDS me to his breast, a feeling so lovely, and I weep as he sings over me:

Me, Mine, she's like Me, and she is Mine.
My sweet, adoring girl.
My clever, wondrous creation, just like Me.
My likeness, My I-am-ness, My lifeness.

I AM my Father's spitting image, a chip off the old block, and hewn from the same Rock. I smell- to be honest – too much of the wild, Son-soaked bliss of Abba's bosom.

I'VE GOT YOU, Papa whispers in my ear.

Come together nice and snug, perfectly shaped and well grown.

This – he touches my chest – *is just skin and bone. It's easy enough to knit back together if you know how.*

We've always been together and always will be. I made it so. Before I knit you, I knew you.

Long before you ever asked Me into your heart, I invited you and formed you in Mine.

I feel his heart for me, and I feel safe,
Safer, the safest I have ever been.

47

THE SHEPHERD HARPEST

The sheep recognize his voice; he calls his sheep by name and leads them out. (He leads them out of the prophetic enclosure – the fold of safety – into life – where my soul is restored in green pastures) (JOHN 10:3).

The lovely Shepherd makes the flock merry in lush, green pastures by playing bucolic psalms.

The songs take you to a place where the wind comes from, and music grows like roses. He plays songs from out of the bosom of God. The notes burn white and sweet in my heart. They lure me and beckon me to remember my bosom beginning in Love.

. . .

WHEN HE PLAYS, the air fills with honey-colored butterflies that beat their wings in time to the music. I listened thoughtlessly to the light, tender rills and phrases until I seemed to breathe them out of the air and draw them into my bones.

My thoughts were no longer coiled in accusation and condemnation, ready to strike at me. I felt myself relax. I felt high and lifted up.

THE MUSIC FLOWED within like water, touching everything. The harping drifted my thoughts to innocence, and I saw myself without stain for the first time. This gave me such immense joy.

I HAD NOT SEEN nor heard anything lovely in a long time. The Shepherd's eyes held the expressions he must have carried since he watched us all take the shape he had created.

RAISE the song and strike the harp. Send round the shells of joy!

His harp leads into the mystic wonder of Union. The sheep dance and chant the sweetest spirit songs.

Through the magic of music and poetry, we celebrate our likeness redeemed and innocence restored! Our melismas are universal and magical. All the flocks sing together harmoniously, and righteousness is our common note.

Our melodies are bound to effortless Union.

THESE SONGS HEAL, for our lovely Shepherd is a song-healer. He composes songs of incarnation for everyday life. He sings with joy about freedom in the wide-open pasture. He hums, the trees sway, the stones sing, and the flock frolics about merrily.

SING THEM FREE, the Shepherd harpist whispers.
You know the songs of freedom.

THE HARP STRUMS, and I hum. He hands me his harp.

I have the spirit of a troubadour. I feel emotions deeply and identify with people intimately. Something shines in my heart beyond the power of words that can only be communicated in a melody.

Softy and tenderly, the earth responds to Life in me, and I match my voice to the sound of it until we hum in unison, trading notes and coming together.

LOVE GIVES Truth its voice (EPHESIANS 4:15A).

Every heart around us unfolds like a flower. It opens and awakens to Abba's unconditional love. The curse of their own delusion of separation is broken in their waking.

AND THE WHOLE earth sings in unison to the Shepherd harpist.

We are his, and we know his voice.
And his voice alone is all we know.

OUR SONGS FILL the meadow of the world. A joyous wind ripples through the pasture with promise and hope.

I dared to gaze upon the Shepherd, and the light in his eyes paved a path to my heart. His radiance blazed me unhindered and spilled through my veins until I saw the whole flock aglow with his glory.

NEVER DID I imagine such luminous joy existed. I looked again, and the meadow filled with lilies in every color.

A SONG of delightful and unheard-of praise bursts from my heart like sweet tones. All my thoughts and affection are on you, my Beloved Shepherd. Ravishing beauty and the sublime splendor of the bliss of this grace have me singing.

. . .

THE SHEPHERD POETS and harpists sing in the Selah pastures of wild love and wide open, gracious spaces. The quiet that the spirit experiences with the lovely Shepherd harpist is very sweet. This music is divine and delectable. The mind is rapt in sublime and ethereal melody and sings the delights of everlasting love.

MY LOVELY SHEPHERD Harpist sings songs to remind the flock how delightfully loved we are. He sings of lambs and lilies.

FOR REST

*What a foolish thing it would be if we
should now fail in a similar fashion to
enter into his rest, where we get to celebrate the full consequences of our
redemption. (Why waste another lap in
the same wilderness of unbelief!)*

*His rest celebrates perfection. His work is
complete; the fall of man did not flaw its
perfection (HEBREWS 4:1;3).*

I know a place deeper in the For-Rest where the road ends, and there is a circle of trees. When I walk into the circle, something changes; time slows down, and I can hear the wind cooing and feel it caressing me.

. . .

The colors seem richer here. I stand still and listen. I can hear the Triune voice. My senses are heightened to Union.

I smell something sweet. It smells like a memory, so I open my eyes, and that's when I see Jesus in a pool of light, just standing there watching me. He is shining like gold. His skin and hair are ivory and gold like honeycomb. Colors seem to flow from him like little, silky drifts, swirling ribbons of green, purple, blue, red, orange, yellow, and gold.

He carries his own breeze. I want to look at him forever. Something about him feels old, like a boulder or a tree when it's watched the sun and moon rise over the ages.

He smiles and comes to me. He lifts his hand and touches my cheek. I smell the light sweetness again, making me feel like something brilliant is about to happen. His smile deepens me.

You know Me, he said.

I know all this seems strange to you, but you need to do nothing except breathe My air and drink the purest waters of My being.

Come take off your heavy shoes and feel the wind beneath your feet.

Stay here, and My musicians will play music while you rest and drink. And the birds began to sweetly sing.

HE HELD out a cup filled with fresh water sweeter than the rarest wines. I lifted my hand to the cup, and he breathed *Drink*. I drink, and I see.

BENEATH THE GRACEFUL canopy of towering trees is a crystal clear river gleaming with life.

All who wander to the heart of the For-Rest speak enthralled of trees in eternal bloom. There are branches laden with flowers in all colors, and ripe fruits sweeter than nectar grow abundantly as wildflowers amid the soft grass.

The idyllic perfection of the For-Rest has birds and beasts that lie down in peace together.

I SEE beyond what I see. The wind blows, and it begins to snow little white Dogwood leaves or maybe Bradford pears. As they blow by me, I follow them back to The Beauty of their beauty.

Mighty oaks and redwoods, trees of all species full of life surround me. I stand under these magnificent trees. A hush settles around me. Looking up into the interlacing branches, I feel their inclusion. The inclusion of Union interfacing with our Creator, God.

· · ·

I GENTLY STEP off the beaten path. I move the leaves aside and scoop up a handful of soil. I feel the texture. I smell the fragrance. I feel the Life-giving life in the soil.

OH, look at this little acorn. I hold it in my hand and follow it back to its tree, its beginning.

> How long have you been in thee?
> How many nestlings call you home?
> Owls, woodpeckers, and chickadees.
> What are you growing My tiny seed;
> yellow-billed magpies, white-tailed deer,
> and flying squirrels?
> Growing more than trees, I see!

HOW MANY, like me, will gaze upon your might and take refuge under your emerald wings? I see the Tree of Life in you. Do you see the Tree of Life in me? I give it a quick kiss before I put the acorn back down.

I SEE the beauty of God in creation. I listen to the trees breathing in the For-Rest. Nature has become a huge part of my enjoyment these days. This earth is lush and alive.

· · ·

I'M A CHILD AGAIN, holding my breath in wonder at the enormity of the world and the Union of all things in Christ Jesus. I reach into my soul for the lingering warmth of life and feel a green halo around my heart, and I murmur to Abba, *Thank You.*

AND I BATHE in the For-Rest.

49

SUNRISE

*But then the day dawned, the most
complete culmination of time! The Son
arrived, commissioned by the Father;
his legal passport to the planet was his
mother's womb. In a human body
exactly like ours, he lived his life subject
to the same scrutiny of the law. His
mandate was to rescue the human race
from the regime of the law of performance and announce the revelation of
their true sonship in God*
(GALATIANS 4:4-5).

B
lue hour. I am sweetly loved.
First light. I love you.
Sunrise tiptoes into my room, reminding
me of the Risen Son. The soft golden light licks my
face with gentle kisses of warmth and assurance.

. . .

I LAY in the Son's warmth, and he brightens me. I laugh and giggle and cry a little before I even leave my bed. His love does that. One thousand shadows that once beckoned me disappeared in a single sunbeam. His love does that, too!

I BREATHE the breath of the dawn. It's like a new life. Here, in the speaking stillness, I am raptured. I lose myself for a moment beyond all senses, but I find my life in his and his in mine.

The Life of One, the Life of all. Oh, how sweet this Union!

AND THE SON smiles over every land. He is the sun that warmeth everyone. The Risen Son shines and illuminates the eyes of my mind, and that I am perfectly redeemed in Christ. The day has dawned in my heart.

THE SHIFTING hues of dawn shine through me. The diaphony of the divine is at the heart of a glowing universe (Pierre Teilhard de Chardin).

THE HOLY BOY, full of life, is on the horizon of our

hearts where the earth meets the sky with redemption and righteousness.

I CREST *at dawn with the world in My arms.*
    See and be warmed, says the Son.
    The world becomes brighter in the Son.

> *The grace of God shines as bright as day,*
>   *making the salvation of mankind unde-*
>   *niably visible (*TITUS *2:11).*

I am in the Son. My thoughts prefer Son-lit places. I'm nestled in like he has been made for me. I fit perfectly here, and I'm incarnadine.

*G*O *color the world in blooms and Son, sunshine girl. Go ye into all the world and shine!*

50

CONFESSIONS OF A JUBILANT

*I announce the Jubilee year of the Lord has
come! This is the liberation celebration
of the Lord, embracing humanity home
(LUKE 4:19).*

I t happened that in the year 2023, of the Incarnation of the Son of God, Jesus Christ, when I was fifty years and two months old, a spiritual sweetness inebriated me from within.

The life-giving life to all made me sweet. The ocean of Jubilee erupted within me. I became acutely aware that *no contribution of the flesh could add to the perfection I was and always will be because of this glorious entanglement of Christ in me* (SEE ROMANS 4:19).

I HEAR the sound of children laughing and the clamor of sumptuous celebrations in my heart.

I hear the Tritoned voice of my dearest Darling, laughing on the waves of grace rolling on this ocean of love and life within my soul.

AT FIFTY, I have been consumed by rapturous love and shall never be the same. Love is my breath, my life, my jubilation, my glory, and my constant delight.

Deeper still, this Jubilant is knowing love's most delicious presence. Abba has chosen me for his permanent dwelling.

It's as if someone has tucked me into the center of Christmas and given me a gazillion gifts. I just keep unwrapping this gift of seamless Union.

JUBILEE IS a divine ecstatic state that is eternal and effortless all because of our love-union in Christ. All frontiers, borders, and hinterlands lead to the ecstasy of Oneness and effortless Union.

The Jubilant speaks of an overflowing radiance of an infinite expanse, a wide-open space of infinitely brilliant light. She speaks of the unity of all things, of a wonderfully and ineffable uplifting of heart.

THE JUBILANT IS MORE FULLY alive than ever, more she than ever, yet at the same time, her ego has been undone.

She knows of immense peace, and God is her

portion. Who needs a double portion when you have all? Have you heard the ecstatic confessions of a Jubilant?

> *The Spirit of the Lord is upon me because*
> *he has anointed me to announce glad*
> *tidings to a starving people; he has*
> *commissioned me to announce the*
> *freedom of forgiveness [their true I-am-*
> *ness] to those held captive at spear-point*
> *by their guilt and shame; also, the blind*
> *may now look up and be restored in*
> *their sight! I am anointed to send out*
> *those who are bruised and traumatized*
> *into the freedom of their redeemed inno-*
> *cence (LUKE 4:18).*

The darling Jubilant sees that love is the broth of life. And she drinks and sees Christ, the Anointed One, in all and knows we are all anointed.

51

THE WAY OF KISSING

... Since I arrived, she hasn't stopped kissing my feet with affection. Jesus said to her, Your kisses perfectly realized your salvation (LUKE 7:45, 50).

The veil is removed from the bride and thrown over the abyss in her mind. With one kiss, she sees nothing but pure Unity.

The boundless love of the bridegroom absorbs and consumes all he holds in his graceful embrace. Nothing left but the grace of Oneness.

INTO THE ETERNAL love I go, which leads me about in the boundless breadth, and I bathe in it. I flow more myself than ever in ecstatic delights amid the treasures of divine affection.

I live and move and have my being in Triune kisses.

I am loved. I am love. I burn, I melt, and I am absorbed in the wonder of this eternal and infinite agape love. Oh, it's other-centered. Just ask the one smothered in kisses.

ABBA WASHED my mind of first Adam with the whisper of I-am-ness. He kissed me on the forehead and, in an ancient tongue, gently whispered to my mind. I felt warmth in my brain, like warm water going in and holding my mind in a warm bath.

One kiss from his honeyed lips answered all the questions that seemed to hum in my beehive brain. He quieted the storm in my mind. I feel an uncustomary moment of pure elation from my fears. This iridescent feeling of euphoria is going to be my new normal. His lips unravel my worries. My grimace becomes a grin.

WHISPERS AND KISSES. Lots of kisses. He loves me so, and this I know. He holds me close to kiss me. And he snuggles me and laughs. He holds me up again to kiss me.

His eyes gleam with a hint of his power and plan. It's so easy to believe him. I see, so I kiss him.

ABBA COVERS me in sugar that I did not earn. Lots and lots of sugar. His breath smells of milk, and I am drunk. He is the light of my life, the breath in my breast, the sun to my world, and the pep in my step.

He crowns my life with smiles. He crowns my life with kisses. Kindled by kisses, our romance is blossoming and burning bright.

I melt with divine love, and I'm hooked on kisses. His kisses have made me unfailingly kind and prone to love.

I SEE the Son in everyone and greet him with kisses. I kiss foreheads and cheeks and hands and feet. I've grown in tenderness and affection. I've been kissed by Love, only to kiss with Love.

I've decided to love the Son in everyone, which, to my delight, requires much cuddling and affection. There is much endearing to be tended to. I tend to the Most Adorable Majesty in all.

Out of these earthly bonds I slip, and lay my ear against your lips. He always seals things with a kiss.

52

MY SWEETING

I am completely engaged in the loveliness of
that which is of exceedingly great value
(2 CORINTHIANS 5:9).

Good morning, My Sweeting.
I have poured the treasure of My sweetness
into all humanity. I have given all that is most
splendid to My Son, and he has shared it with his friends
(Henry Suso).

LET sweetness be overcome by sweetness. The divine
sweetness of Abba's wondrous nature within me makes
me sweet and fruity. I study beautifulness and
sweetness.

I've found a hidden treasure trove of sweetness in
the Silver Sneakers Sunday School class at Destin

Methodist Church. They have tasted of life and love, and sorrow and grief, and are sticky-sweet.

CHRIST SWEETENS my life through people. We are the sweet, savory charms of his endearment. I delight in the divine sweetness. O joys, Infinite Sweetness, Almighty love has unleashed the power of love in my life. I am the target of arrows of love from the sweetness of His divine heart. There is no restraining the excess of Abba's sweetness.

I SHALL NEVER REFUSE her anything she wants of Me. The ardor of the love in her heart causes Me to inwardly melt. And as fat melts the fire, so the sweetness of My divine heart melted by the warmth of her love falls drop by drop continually into her soul (Henry Vaughn).

I CALL HIM HONEY-MOUTH. O wind, O Mighty Breath, You breathe in me forgotten things from before I was in my mother's womb and from the Oneness, outside of time. I sip from anouthen realities and find myself sweet.

He is Honey-mouth, the Rose of the World, and The Mystery hidden in mankind. O sweetness of sweetness, I love Thee.

. . .

I AM FASCINATED WITH YOU. My fluttering soul is high on kisses from Honey-mouth. His truest treasure is the sweetness of his face, kind enough for kissing. Kiss and see.

HAPPY IS she who tastes and sees the One she loves.

I DRINK some honied wine for weariness. A fiery tingling rushed through my body, and some of my exhaustion immediately lifted. This honied wine has the most delicious presence in mind.

I'm sticky-sweet from the land of honey. I drink the nectar of his love, and instantly, I'm abuzz with the finished works of Christ.

Like busy bees working my whole life for me, and I didn't know it. I'm like the girl who carried the beehive. The bees did all the work, and I sweetly enjoyed this honey-drenched life.

I'M ENGULFED in Christ's sweetness and enjoying the ecstasy of our effortless Union. He did our part.

MY GOD, my Life, my Cure. Where I once felt judgment and suspicions, now I feel nuzzled and secure. He crowns my life with sweetness.

· · ·

His words became a transforming nectar to my wounded soul. Sweet awareness by the amazing grace of the presence of Christ alive within me (Walt Whitman).

I take my fill of love and beauty and am filled with the rapture and sweetness of the Godhead dwelling within my temple (St. Symeon the New Theologian).

I lay in the overflowing comfort and sweetness with my eyes closed in the enjoyment of God. My soul delights in the enjoyment of God (Mechtild Von Hackborn).

It was the sweetness of eternal life that burst forth when we stared at each other face to face. This overpowering entrancement is eternal life. When I came to myself, I felt in every way like one who had come from another world. My soul is filled with heavenly wonder. I float and emit a sweet, heavenly fragrance (Gertrude of Hefta).

When she hears songs of praise or sweet music, or strings or songs of temporal love being sung or said, her mind and heart are suddenly, with a detached inward gaze, led into her precious sweetheart, from whom all love flows (Henry Suso).

. . .

HE GIVES me streams of sweetness. He has bedewed me with the dew of Divinity (Christina Ebner).

HE HAS BEEN ESPECIALLY gracious to me. He has worked the miracle of sweetness in me. The favor of God has increased my heart with unspeakable sweetness.

I speak now with no one so much as Thee. (Ahahh-hahah). My garment is bliss. The sweetness of my beauty is the greatness of his love. He reconciles all things in sweetness. He is the original outflow of all honey. This unspeakable sweetness is diffusing, unifying, and transforming the world.

SING YOUR HONEYED SONG. Taste these heavenly treats that gladden and gleam with eternal glory.

OH, this interior sweetness is making my soul fat and sticky with delight. This sweet doctrine of union and inclusion is making my soul a bakery of the savoriest delights (Mechthild of Magdeburg).

THE LOVELINESS and beauty of Abba's grace have sweetened my soul and made me incapably drunk under his influence. He promises to make me drunk from the rivers of intoxicating pleasure.

His words drop into my ears like beeswax, deafening and sweet. The air around him is sweet and heavy with honey.

Sweet is the Voice of promise, and soft is the kiss of the warming Son. I am deep in the honey sweetness of Abba's love. My thoughts are mind-full of the sweetness of resurrection life, likeness redeemed, and innocence restored.

53

UNFLINCHING FLAME

*L*ove is the greatest thing in all the world. Listen to what love is speaking. Only love can teach the art of loving. The Spirit makes it known to us. The heart knows what the mind can never grasp (Francois du Toit).

I'VE NEVER ONCE HEARD Abba say a cruel thing about anyone. He is notorious for love with no conditions. He is famous for his unflinching acceptance and unwavering support. Everything is a matter of love. Everything shall be purified in the fiery ocean of his love.

I AM DRAWN by the electric energy of his love and caught in the spell of love's ecstasy. Immersed evermore into a sea of glass mingled with fire. This lake of fire shall purify all minds from performance and self-effort.

EVERYTHING about his love speaks of his mission accomplished in saving the whole world. The world is a burning bush full of the presence of I Am.

Perfectly aflame in this love, I am as I should be. I feel as if I am made of flames. I close my eyes and yield to the lake of fire. Rage and fear melt when face to face with love.

HERE, let Me give the fire of My love a little wind and see what happens.

It feels like a warm breath that sweeps through me. I can see the light shining through my skin, making a pleasing lantern of my body. I am shining like the Son. I breathe while I burn. With every breath, I grow brighter and hotter. I can see my bones glowing and my marrow like flowing lava.

Abba's wrapped me in his arms, and I am no longer heavy. I no longer dread being alone with my thoughts and memories. I bask in the warmth of his joy. He has the warm, kind presence of a friend who sits with you for comfort and loves you no matter what.

IT MAKES Me glad to be with you.

. . .

I FLOAT UP AS A SPARK. There is no weight to me. I burn, I melt, absorbed in wonder eternally and infinitely. I fly into Abba's open mouth and revel in Our likeness and innocence in the depth of my being.

I AM a priestess of the Flame and a lover of the Eternal Ember. I gaze into the fire and see faces in the flames. The fire of his love claims me as his Daughter, and the illusion of any separation is engulfed. This love is uncomplicated, and We are One.

54

FIRSTLING OF JOY

I *happy am. Joy is my name*
Sweet joy, sweet joy,
Pretty joy,
Sweet joy, sweet joy,
Joy smiles, Laughing joy
Constant joy (William Blake).

HE IS the Firstling of joy, and we are his joy springs.

ME, Lord?
Callest me Thy joy, Thy love, Thy treasure?
Yes, My daughter of sweet, sweet smiles.
Me, Lord?
Of these love glances, those kindling eyes?
Yes, My daughter of utopian grace-giggles.
Us, Lord?

The center of your joy?

Yes, loves, and the fountains, in which I have placed of My nectar.

MY JOY IS my defense of the Gospel. There's no need for apologetics when you can smile. I'm not trying to prove anything or convince anyone. My smile gives attractive evidence of Christ's life within.

SUPREME SPIRITUAL PLEASURE in my soul comes from the joy of his love. He delights in revealing himself to me. His face is alight with delight.

THIS FEELING IS SO joyful and full of goodness that I feel peaceful, easy, and at rest. Nothing can separate me from this eternal love bliss that is my very existence and being.

JESUS IS MY BLISS. Oh, the blissful heights of His love. His joy ripples through me like the rush of cool living water, light and bubbly and startling in intensity.

JOY IS the native tongue of the Gospel. The nature of the Gospel is eternal gladness (Benjamin Dunn).

Our joy is the joy of salvation from the DIY mentality of the law of performance.

WHEN HE HAD FILLED me with heavenly joy, he lifted me up and seated me on his throne with him. I kiss the light of his countenance. He enlightens and mystically teaches me from joy (St. Symeon the New Theologian).

HE GLADDENS and widens my heart, and opens my soul for me, and unlocks it with divine mercies. I am glad of God. He is mine, and I am his (Else von Neustadt).

OH, soul, you are perfect – Rejoice! (Mechthild of Magdeburg).

I AM CONVINCED of Abba's delight in me and high on the majesty of God. There's never a moment I am not engulfed, no, not one.

55

LOVE DRUNK

While wine offers no lasting escape from the
evil of the day, spirit certainly does!
Indulge in spirit intoxication
(EPHESIANS 5:18).

She is wondrous deep in the cups and spills the secrets of love once she's drunk. She's tasted a liquor from a heavenly tap, never brewed by man's hands. Drunken laughter makes her fly. She's so high on divine love.

SHE IS HOOKED ON GOD. She's found her purpose: a trophy wife indeed, ravished and lavished upon the sea of blissful awareness in the waves of ecstatic love. She's free to giggle.

. . .

ABBA IS the fountain of all bliss, and we drink straight from The Vine. Oh, the tenderness of The Vine makes me divinely sweet. The sweeter the grapes, the stronger the wine.

GOD POURS me out the host's own wine, which he himself has drunk. From this wine, I become so overpowered that what the spirit then sings inwardly, sounds sweeter by far than any earthly song (Mechthild of Magdeburg).

I AM INTOXICATED with love's cup – the worlds have passed from my mind. I see within me an overturned cup. I feel a limitless happiness in my being, filling every nook and cranny with your love (St. Symeon the New Theologian).

ABBA IS the keeper of the wine cellar. He makes her life sweet. Her mouth overflows with strong drink. She is an ambassador of the brew of the dew of heaven. She's top shelf and eloquently aged to perfection. How sweet her life is cannot be put into words.

ABBA IS EVEN MORE tasty in people. Each one is a divine drink, a secret sip. Each time we join in fellowship, we experience an intoxicating feast in a festival for the soul. We enjoy the warm charm of human persons.

Each person is a fresh vintage, a bottle waiting to be sipped and enjoyed.

DRUNKS DON'T CARE what people say about them. They don't even remember sin.

She woke up from a love-drunken stupor and didn't know where she was, but it was warm and bright. It felt like she was in a hug, and she couldn't remember what sin was. May we experience a *blackout* of the most divine ideal.

DRUNK WITH THE *new wine of love, I am*
    Drunk as the wild bee in the flowery meadow
    Every flower has become a breast for the love-drunk bee, singing her mad sweet vibe.
    Drunk, drunk with love, I am.
    Born aloft and milk drunk on my beloved.
    (St. John of the Cross).

THE ENRICHMENT and ferment of this honeyed wine is divinely all-inclusive. Drunk with love and all inhibitions gone, the whole world is a lover's lane.

SO BEAUTIFUL THE *face of Him I love.*
    All his body is so filled with light.
    Bounded by love, the cosmos inside.

So drunk am I with adoration,
No longer have I any need of commonplace intoxication.
The common wine has lost its taste,
Now grace, grace, grace, oh satiates.
Poured out from heaven's Son.
Drink it freely, everyone (Henry Suso).

56

PHOTINI

Jesus responded to her, So here I am
speaking to you! I am the One you were
longing for (JOHN 4:26).

Meet me at Lover's Well in the heat of the day, and I will cool your sweaty brow and soothe your soul.

Oh, the well of wonder. The Savior is aware of the deepest longings of our hearts. Whatever our deepest pain or reputation in the community, Jesus sees us and loves us. The living water he offers is more than just a way to have your thirst quenched. It's a new way of life.

PHOTINI DRANK AND WAS DRENCHED. Her longing for love was fulfilled. She grinned, maybe for the first time in a long time. Love bubbled in her belly. She saw something in his eyes she had never seen before, and it changed her.

How did you find him? They asked.

He found me, she said.

What kind of Messiah is this? He searches for bandits, half-breeds, and those who have rejected the prophets and the psalms. Those who only read the books of the law. Those who were living together unwed. They're the talked about, the laughed at, the ones who didn't know the Bible.

He chose the unchosen (AHAHAHA). The imperfect, worshipping their own mountain group of generational heathens. They are the ones who have a history of paganism, child sacrifice, and sex offenders. Religion has excluded them, a sorry bunch whose forefathers had intermarried and soiled the race.

And God goes off the beaten path to find them.

And he stays with them!

He tried to go unnoticed, incognito – but he

couldn't help himself when he saw her. She was weary, too. They shared a moment, a weary moment.

WE'RE IN THIS TOGETHER.

HE WAS DYING to tell someone He was the Savior of the World. *Exclusion over, I am here to include you, your people, and the rest of the world in My saving plan. I am the Messiah. I am the One you've been waiting for.*

AND SHE DRANK straight from the Vine, the mouth of God, the eye of the Fount of Life. And she awoke.

PHOTINI IS the minister of drink. We drink again each time we tell her story, our story of inclusion. The tiny tickling sound of fresh, running water in a cold well comes to greet you each time she draws near. And the drink is so deep, like an ancient chimney from Abba's deep, deep bosom.

THE WELL ISN'T A PLACE. It's a dimension of Union and inclusion. It is a sense of well-being and fulfillment.

. . .

ALL IS WELL, and all shall be well, and all manner of thing shall be well (Julian of Norwich).

SHE LOVES. He is love.
   She is thirsty. He is a fountain
   (Bernard of Clairvaux).

57

BRIGHT EYES SET HIS SIGHT ON ME

B lue streams, fields green,
        Thoughts echo upland.
        Here I am, honey bunny,
We dance in bee-loud meadows.

BRIGHT EYES SET his sight on me.
    Lift off, lift off,
    I fly in him.
    Light eyes, Light eyes
    Six eyes, Three faces, one Lamb, I Am.
    Daughter, daughter, daughter,
    Son of God.

DARLING, darling, darling,
    Dear, dear, dear,
    Oh, so dear to me. Oh, so darling, see!

All humankind is all Godkind.
Three in One, the World in Son.
Bright eyes seated, all accomplished.

I FOLLOW *the dazzling trail of the sublime beauty and harmony I see in your eyes. Your eyes have lit the lamp in my soul. And in my soul, I have found a single point on a person, your person, Jesus* (Pierre Teilhard de Chardin).

LIGHT AND LIFE to all he brings.

An energy hangs in the air between us and tethers me to Christ. Everything around me has become the substance of his heart. When I look at him, calm floods over my thoughts like smoke over a beehive.

I instantly sense that he knows why people are hurting, and he cares. Kindness never leaves his gaze. No one has ever shown me this kind of tenderness. With a flash of a smile, he walks through the walls of my heart. My heart has always been his home.

DON'T LOOK AT THEM. *Look at Me.* His eyes speak, and his voice is morning bright.

EVERYTHING about the Risen Christ shines. There is a subtle shimmer about him, like the way the heat rises from the pavement in the summer in little waves. I am smitten. Looking at Christ is necessary to me. It is essential.

HE LAUGHS, and his face is bright with victory. Warm, rich colors flash everywhere out of him. Light pours from him like the brightest day. He's so bright I am nearly blinded but can't turn away. I am mesmerized and captivated by the features of his face.

HE CAN'T LOOK AWAY, either. What is it about us humans that so captivates his gaze? He has set his affection on us. He sees his likeness redeemed and innocence restored in humanity.

He sees himself in me, righteous and all innocent and glowing in otherworldly radiance.

ENLIGHTENED ONE, you glow like Us, like Godkind.

BRIGHT EYES SET his sight on the world.

58

THE EMBRACING MIRROR

And we all, with new understanding, see
ourselves in him as in a mirror. In him,
every face is unveiled. Every feature of
his image articulated in Christ is
reflected within us! The Spirit of the
Lord engineers this radical transforma-
tion; we are led from an inferior mind-
set to the revealed endorsement of our
authentic identity
(SEE 2 CORINTHIANS 3:18).

W hen he holds me, I feel comfort not of this world. Words leave my mind. The moment we embrace a light of divine love bonds his heart to me and mine to him. And standing in the eternal embracing mirror, I learn who He is without tongue or words better than if we had spoken with lips or language. I cannot attempt to explain in sounds what I felt within.

How wonderful the Mirror's embrace. I am drunk on love forever after this (*The Embracing Mirror*, Mechthild of Magdeburg).

I GRIN at myself in the mirror. I look like the Son.

I am a son of God, I whisper. It sounds so scandalous. My skin tingles and glows a little, and I know it's true.

HE IS the only Man I know who gives mirrors to blind people so they may see who they are.

BEHOLD THE LORD *is our mirror.*
   Open your eyes and see them in Him,
   And learn the manner of your face
   (Ode 13, *The Odes of Solomon*).

I AM a living mirror on which the Father, Son, and Spirit have poured truth. I am mesmerized and captivated by Christ in me. I turn to walk away, but I don't get far. I have to look again. *Is this real life?*

> *Now, with unveiled faces, we are gazing at*
>   *the glory of the Lord as in a mirror, and*
>   *metamorphe happens – image and like-*
>   *ness awaken within us*

(2 CORINTHIANS 3:18 COMMENTARY,
Francois du Toit).

I hear giggles and see glistening eyes.

ABBA HAS PROGRAMMED *and encoded light deep within the*
marrow of our DNA to reflect his perfection, and it's as
effortless as breathing. To reflect anything else is a mere
disruption, a disfiguration, a distorted, blurry mirror image.
It would be unrest (Keisha Holder, The Mirror Word
Bible Study Group, Facebook).

AT REST, like still waters, I seamlessly reflect I Am. I
cannot look away from him in me, and me in him –
flawless, Oneness, I-am-ness, and immaculately beautiful and innocent.

I rest in the full consequences of redemption. I'll
try to walk away again, but I know I'll be back to gaze
at our seamless Union.

I SPIN AROUND three times and smell the air. I am
exactly where I should be. I am exactly who I ought to
be. Christ's manifest likeness is mirrored in me! Our
sameness cannot be compromised or contradicted.

.   .   .

OH, My darling, look at us, looking at each other and loving one another.

> *By the waters of reflection, I remember who*
> *I am (PSALM 23, Francois du Toit).*

I have found a sea of glass where the reflection is quite exquisite. This reflection calmed a storm in me and soothed my soul forever.

I have found a sea of glass mingled with fire. In the flames of this fire, you cannot tell the difference between Our faces. We are One. The fire blazes with Union.

MY OLD THOUGHTS OF SEPARATION, striving, and failure ceased. They went away. And now, my mind endorses our Union, and my authentic likeness redeemed, and innocence restored.

59

UNDERSTAND OUR UNION YET?

*For anyone to see and to say that Jesus is
the Son of God is to awaken to the
awareness that we are continuously,
seamlessly joined in oneness*
(1 JOHN 4:15).

Familiar verses sparkle anew when read through the lens of Union and joint participation. Christ exists in all things and dwells in everyone.

I BELIEVE IN ONENESS. The heart of the gospel is the nitty-gritty essence of Oneness. The gospel is universal and addressed to all because we are One (Julian of Norwich).

. . .

THE STATE of the Union is the effortless, inseparable seamlessness that we have always been one with the Godhead. In the silence and sweetness, he shows me our eternal Oneness. We have always been One. I may have forgotten for a time, but really, I didn't. I knew. I just didn't know what I was looking for.

STAY in the place of nothing.
  Nothing to do,
  Nothing to say.
  Just to know, We have always been together.
  We have never been separated (Lydia du Toit).

YOU ARE ACQUAINTED WITH ME, remember? You know Me. Your subconscious thoughts are anchored in eternal Union forever. Nothing you have ever done or could ever do has what it takes to separate us.

EVERY ASPECT of your life already gives eloquent expression to the rich reservoirs of your Union in him. You certainly have the testimony of Jesus evidenced in you (Francois du Toit).

HE IS PLEASED to reveal our Oneness and show the extent of his love.

I am wired and alert to treasure our
Oneness (see EPHESIANS 4:3).

Realize your strength in the Master; your
union with him is your limitless
resource (EPHESIANS 6:10).

I've been brought to the point where I can no longer see anything nor any longer breathe outside that milieu in which all is made effortlessly One. I'm plunged into the all-inclusive One, the One so perfect that I lose myself in the ultimate perfection of my own individuality (Pierre Teilhard de Chardin).

OH, this glorious Union. Steep yourself in I-am-ness, Abbaness, Oneness. Enjoy Union, for it is your source of life and youthfulness. The inexpressible relationship Abba brought us into is divine and meant to be experienced.

True Union doesn't stifle, confuse, or conform. It super-differentiates us to be beautifully free in the perfection of agape.

I SEE in ever more dazzling and consistent form the essence of Abba enveloping all. As I ponder Union, a supernatural sense of the divine flows through me with a natural sense of plentitude.

Suddenly, I am aware that I am full of God. What a

relief! This incredible love radiates from me as I overflow in the understanding of our Union.

If nothing can diminish Abba, then nothing can diminish me. I am irreducible, undiminishable, and un-belittlable. I am fundamentally irreducible because I am irreducibly united with Father, Son, and Spirt. Effortlessly and without distortion, the Trinity upholds our Union.

> *The one whose idea you are, to begin with,*
> *designed you to radiate his image and*
> *likeness; he is the true pattern of your*
> *beingness! So be who you are in real-*
> *izing the exact details of your genesis!*
> *You are whole and in perfect harmony;*
> *seamlessly one with him*
> (*I Peter 1:15*).

She is another Me, made so by the Union of Love (Catherine of Siena).

60

JESUS

I have come with the sole purpose for you to
have life in its most complete form
(JOHN 10:10B).

I love this Man who healed me with a touch and has no hint of anger in his eyes. He's saved my life more times than I can count.

He finds all my secret fears and carries them away one by one. His love cannot be induced or dissuaded. He loves me no matter what.

YOU ARE MY EXCEPTIONAL MAN, Jesus.

Your life echoes redeemed likeness and restored innocence within my own life. Oh, Life of my life, you are the Life-giving life to all. Surely, you are the Way, the Truth, and the Life.

. . .

MY HEART KNOWS HIM. When I look at him, sometimes I see flames that turn into something golden. His eyes reflect a love so immense that it holds my backbone together.

I SAY HIS NAME, *Jesus*, and something in his eyes gleam with sheer delight. His is the sweetest name I know.

Rachael, he says. And he lifts his hand to meet mine. When he said my name, I recognized myself in him.

You are with me here, and he tapped his fingertips to his heart. *Long before you invited me into your heart, I asked you into Mine. I'm in you, and you are in Me.*

I BELONG HERE IN HIM. My bones know it.

HE COMES to me in every dark place, and in every memory, he is there. His eyes hold mine. They know me.

When he looks at me, there is strength in his eyes, and I take some of it for myself. He looks at me like he knows I'm stronger than I might seem.

HE HAS THE WARM, kind presence of a friend who would sit by you through the darkest of nights. He has gone into my darkest nightmare and faced my cruelest judgment. He has died my death.

We're in this together, he said. I find his love and presence to be ravishing.

He moves with a strange delicacy and grace, as if he is close to dancing. He's as lovely as a warm wind on a cool day. He uses an indulgent tone with me.

Taken me under his wing, has he! It's like a fresh nest fitted for new beginnings. My dearest sees me and holds up his wing, always only inviting me under.

He initiated our relationship.

I've always been his. I've always been in him. I believe in and experience our Union.

He longs for me to sit with him and enjoy his company. He starts a fire. Imagine royal hands collecting wood and making breakfast for his loves. Picture the grin on his face as he cooks.

He seems no more than a handsome, hot-hearted, intelligent, untaught carpenter until you see his eyes and smile. Nothing in books can explain how the beauty of his face can heal a hurting heart.

I DELIGHT in his searching gaze. He searches my heart for himself and finds eternity there, and his Father. Jesus reveals that I pre-existed in God. That makes us kin and family forever.

Everything about him seems ordinary to the naked eye, yet he vibrates with an outpouring of the raw energy of love. The air around him is filled with promise. He is to be felt more than seen.

JESUS PROVES that there is such a thing as a free lunch. Bread magically appears carried on raven's wings and money in the mouths of mullets. There are gifts with no strings attached.

AROUND TWO THOUSAND YEARS AGO, I entered heaven when Jesus died and ascended with me in his arms. He's tucked me into the privatest of places.

I HAVE SEEN what you want, and he is here.
  A Beloved of infinite tenderness
  (Catherine of Siena).

61

PLEROMIC BLOSSOMS

*He is the head; the Ekklesia is his body. The
completeness of his being that fills all in
all resides in us. God cannot make
himself more visible or exhibit himself
more accurately (EPHESIANS 1:23).*

I cannot wrap my mind around this divine fullness and completeness. This inward sense of plentitude, fullness, and eternal communion invigorates and intoxicates my life.

My dear-hart no longer pants for the water as I have found all of God is satisfied to live in me.

EVERYTHING from here on is simply the story of unveiling the pleroma within.

In him, all the fullness of Deity resides in a

> *human body. He proves that human life*
> *is tailor-made for God. God is fully at*
> *home in us (COLOSSIANS 2:9).*

I live in this dynamic sense of plentitude. I feel the inward glow of satisfaction as Abba whispers from deep within me, *We love living here.*

THE SENSE of plentitude comes from knowing and endlessly enjoying the awareness of Christ in me. It's a sense of completion, consummation, and consumption. I'm filled with the fullness of God and I couldn't get any fuller. I am conscious of our Union.

> *Separation is an illusion. Oneness was God's*
> *idea all along! He desires to express*
> *himself through our touch, our voice,*
> *and our presence. He is so happy to*
> *dwell in us! There is no place in the*
> *universe where he would rather be.*
> *(EPHESIANS 3:19 COMMENTARY,*
> *Francois du Toit).*

Our awareness of his indwelling grows richer, purer, and more beautiful than language can express.

ALL THINGS ARE IN HIM, *and all things find their fulfillment in him. We live and act immersed in this living atmosphere co-extensive with the world in fullness. Everything is incarnate.*

Christ is not something added to the world as an extra. He is not an embellishment. He is the Alpha and Omega, the principle and the end, the foundation and the keystone, the plentitude and the plentifier.

It is he who fills all things. In no instance in the world is there any element of the world that has moved, that moves, or ever shall move, outside the directing flood he pours into; space and duration are filled by him (Pierre Teilhard de Chardin).

ALL CREATED things are so very full of God. He is the center that fills the whole sphere. The omnipresence of God is in all.

Let's leave the surface and plunge into God. In our depths, we find his divine nature, that Incorruptible Seed of God that has always been implanted here within our souls.

WE ARE PLEROMIC BLOSSOMS. The affection of the Trinity is so great within that we shall explode with love and drench the world.

> *I desire for you to become intimately*
> *acquainted with the love of Christ on*
> *the deepest possible level, far beyond the*
> *reach of a mere academic, intellectual*

grasp. Within the scope of this equation,
God finds the ultimate expression of
himself in you (EPHESIANS 3:19).

Oh, this sense of plentitude branching from the ever-loving Vine within shall surely be the life of me. I am effortlessly full of Christ and a perpetually blooming branchling.

62

THE ILLUSTRATED MAN

For in him we live and move and have our being, as even some of your own poets have said, For we are indeed his offspring (ACTS 17:28, English Standard Version).

I was walking on the beach yesterday when I met the Illustrated Man.

He opened his hand, and on his palm was a rose freshly cut with drops of crystal water among the crimson petals.

I put my hand out to touch it and felt ecstatic love and immense joy. It was alive, and I could smell it.

HE TOOK HIS SHIRT OFF. He was covered with illustrations all over his body. I see the crowds that inhabit his body. I hear their voices, small and quiet. He sounds like a walking waterfall.

Funny, he said, *I can feel every one of them all at the same time.*

WE SAT DOWN, and I cannot say how I stared at him, for he was a jubilee of rockets and fountains and people in such detail and color that you hear the voices murmuring small from the crowds that inhabited his body.

When his flesh twitched, their tiny mouths flickered, their eyes winked, and a tiny pink hand waved at me.

THERE WERE yellow meadows and blue rivers and mountains and stars and the sun and the planets. Spread across his chest is the Milky Way, like a sash.

The people themselves were in groups on his arms, shoulders, back, sides, and wrists. They were in the forests of his hair, his freckles, and his beard. They were appearing from his armpit caverns with their diamond eyes a glitter.

Each had their own activity, and each had its own unique portrait, and they were all united in him. It was infinitely detailed, and when he moved, they moved, but they could move uniquely within him.

· · ·

HERE, on One gathered wall, were all the finest scenes of the cosmos. The colors burned in many dimensions. He was like a window looking into a fiery reality. The man was a walking world, a treasure gallery, a human globe.

This was not a cheap work of art. This was the accomplishment of a genius. A living, vibrant, clear, and beautiful picture of love, union, and of Incarnation.

The sun set, and in the moonlight, the Illustrated Man's pictures glowed like charcoals in the half-light, like scattered rubies and emeralds, like Picasso colors along his outstretched body.

Each illustration is a little story, part of the big story. If you watch them in a few minutes, they tell you a tale. It's all here; just waiting for you to see and hear it.

IN THE LIGHT, I see him grinning. I watch him as he muses over and marvels at the finished work on his body. His amber eyes twinkle and little pools form and glisten.

I watch as he folds his arms, cradling all humanity within himself. Then he looks back at me and winks.

(PORTIONS FROM *THE ILLUSTRATED MAN*, by Ray Bradbury)

63

FACE TO FACE

And you will gaze upon him, face to face;
recognizing every distinct detail of his
divine features mirrored in you! His
Name will find a face in you
(REVELATION 22:4).

He has the loveliest face I've ever seen.

The sun rises on his face. How do I not melt away in the radiance of his face? I'm flooded with waves of euphoria, and it feels like I am breathing new air.

Oh, how I love you, little lamb.

All is paid.

All is paid.

Your face refreshed Me, My love.

.   .   .

My Beloved smiled when he said it, and I felt my wings open and fly.

The truest treasure is the sweetness of his face, kind enough for kissing and lit with affection and approval. Nothing in books can explain how the beauty of his face can heal a hurting heart. Each time I think of the image of his face, I think of a celebration, like I might have linked to the feeling of receiving a wonderful gift.

We face each other. Abba puts his hands on my shoulders and says, *You are safe now.* The gentleness in his voice startles me, and I stare. He noticed me watching.

Seems familiar, doesn't it? I have many faces, and I might be anyone you meet anywhere.

He smiled and kissed my heart and kindled it to flame and then to poetry. The warmth of his smile spread through my heart and healed me. In his smile, I see myself living the life he's envisioned for me.

His smile is like a light that catches me and clings to me. I keep looking at his face. I learn by looking. I'm a wild child living close to his face. He lets me run wild.

· · ·

I MUST DESCRIBE the features of the resplendent image that has been disclosed to me and whose face I hold now in my very human hands (Mechtild of Magdeburg).

YOUR FACE so full of graciousness.
> *Your mouth so full of living words.*
> *The tenderness of love continues to astound me.*
> *The paternity of your Abbaness is my existence.*
> *Wonderful and dazzling in brightness.*
> *The entire delight of my soul* (Henry Suso).

64

FREE AS A BIRD

Christ defines your faith; he is your freedom
from anything from which the law
could never free you! Find your firm
footing in this freedom. Do not let reli-
gion trip you up again and harness you
to a system of rules and obligations
(GALATIANS 5:1).

I survived the Great Inquisition of the 21st-century church. It's still the same old system. Since the upholders of the law cannot physically burn your body, they burn your character instead.

Once I was freed from Adam's ribcage and shockingly without friends or family to guide me, the Spirit of Truth so sweetly found me.

A wild, free, luscious, and green pasture awaits you outside of the coffin of religion. The loveliness of what I've found to be true has set me free. I'll never go back.

To come back into the pen would be exile. The taste of freedom is sweet and oh-so full of life.

How can a bird born for joy sit in a cage and sing?

FIND your firm footing in this freedom. Christ Jesus is our Liberator, and he has set us free.

Freedom is the law of perfect love. It's love that has been embroidered, entwined, and interfaced in our hearts. The law of love liberates us into a different lifestyle.

I'VE BEEN LOVED into the place of freedom by the Father, Son, and Holy Spirit (Matt Spinks, *Kainos Koinonia*, Facebook).

IN CHRIST, we are all equally free. The ransom he paid for my freedom binds me to him in the sweetest of all sweetness and to the lordship of his love. There's a euphoric unspooling in my mind as the Truth sets me free.

Jesus was bent on winning freedom for the entire world. So, be free from the bondage of all things and free those who are bound.

WHAT'S the point of all this glorious freedom if we don't enjoy it?

．　．　．

MY CAGE DAYS ARE OVER, and I'm so free I fly. I'm smiling so big, and my eyes glisten in the wind. I've been a free bird for about a year now. I have these beautiful new feathers, and life feels grand. I effortlessly river the air. I prefer weightless days and green pastures the size of the world.

Pretty soon, I'll need more world to explore.

THE LOVE of God is the air she breathes. It is not a discipline or practice but life itself. It's breathing Love's breath. She is profoundly conscious of this love that moves through her constantly (Mechthild of Magdeburg).

A FREELING CANNOT BE HELD hostage in a cage of invisible rules or religious protocols of hierarchy that demand honor, which is underhanded control.

WE'VE BEEN RELEASED. No longer pot-bound in a dwarfed existence. Released to live wild and free beyond the four walls of religion. Wide open pastures and luscious green meadows of his love are in your near future.

．　．　．

ON MEDITATIONS of heaven's wings, soaring so free, I breathe imperial air. Of love omnific, omnipotent, and omnipresent. The air warbles as it flows and carries me higher. I am everywhere through eternity all at once. I am a young Yona. Free, oh so free. Wild, oh so wild. I've caught the wind of everywhere (Henry Suso).

65

WORD BATH
IMPARTATION OF ACQUITTAL

His love words bathe us and remove every
stain of sin (see EPHESIANS 5:26).

His words cling to me, and I ponder them at odd moments. I stuff the pockets of my heart with love ponderings for later. They ring in my ears and flash through my mind like light, little shock waves. They cause my bones to bloom.

This same Abba who whispers his love to me has spoken trees, animals, and stars into existence. He's wild for us. He tells me so.

I REMEMBER when the voices of my accusers wrapped around me like a noose. But his voice cut through their words and my thoughts.

The moment I heard his words aloud, the tension deep inside, for all these years, unraveled. A lightness swept through me like a rush of freedom. I hadn't realized the weight of accusation and condemnation until it lifted, and I was free.

HE HELD out his hand like an invitation. Inviting me to walk with him.

I protect you because you mean something to Me.
Agree with My thoughts for you. Take sides with Me.
I uphold the life of your design.

I believe him and know that I am safe. His thoughts envelop me like a living shield. I am in a powerful force field of protecting love.

SIN SPEAKS a dead language that leaves us confused. Papa speaks our native tongue and is easy to understand because he speaks love, the universal language. His words breathe liquid adoration. He has been exceedingly gracious to us.

THE FATHER'S words found us in the dark night, pitch black, and his voice brought his face into perfect view. He spoke, and something deep inside awakened like a memory, and our eyes opened from sleep.

HE CALLED my name in a voice like music. He called me the meaning of my name, *Little lamb*, and it pierced into the depths of my soul. The Tritoned voice was warm, oh, so warm, holding me like a hug from the inside out. I sense I've always known this voice. It rings in my ears and warms my limbs.

DAUGHTER, *Made-of-Me, Mine.*

He said my name, *Rachael.*

And there was a click inside me, like a key in a lock! My heart melted, and I knew instantly who I had always been.

Daughter.

SOMETHING SHIFTED deep within when he spoke, imbuing me with a sense of Oneness as though I had connected with a vital part of myself that I had forgotten. I inhale all the warmth of the memories in his words.

He morphs from a laughing friend to a patient teacher to a kind Father, all the while filled with overwhelming unconditional love.

HIS VOICE IS MADE of gentleness and full of flaming embers and wine. I listen to him, and the darkness dissolves around me. His voice is friendly and soothing. Under his care, my heart shall find healing and happiness. His voice is like a permanent holiday from meetings and meltdowns, cell phones and sciatica, bills and brooms.

I LISTEN to his ancient voice singing a rhapsody from the deepest realm of my soul. His voice is so grand. It makes the land lovely and the earth beautiful. He giggles over us. He loves what he sees.

THE VOICE of the fallen mind grew mute as his voice filled my soul: a deep, lovely, gentle roar like that of a fathomless ocean. It wasn't old or young, neither male nor female. But I knew, without seeing its face, that this voice had made me.

HIS WORD IS life and bread to me. His voice is thick with age and new life. I shall not live by bread alone but by every word that proceeds from the mouth of Abba.

ALTHOUGH WE HAVE WANDERED, the soft hum of his voice has found our bones and called them home. His voice calls his family together from the lowlands to the highlands.

I do not know what helps me more than hearing Abba's voice.

· · ·

LIKE THE SWAY of ocean swelling
Rolled his deep voice 'round my dwelling.
When the Three with soaring chorus
Sing a love song in and o'er us (William Blake).

Salvation is not a reward for good behavior.
It has absolutely nothing to do with
anything that we have done. God's
mercy saved us. The Holy Spirit
endorses in us what happened to us
when Jesus Christ died and was raised!
When we heard the glad announcement
of salvation, it was like taking a deep,
warm bath! Our minds were thor-
oughly cleansed and re-booted into the
newness of life (TITUS 3:5).

66

MAMA DOVE

His own Spirit is the source of this gift of
knowing that we are continuously,
seamlessly, and very consciously
present in him, and he in us
(1 JOHN 4:13).

The breath I breathe is full of divine life. Spirit, I trust her. She is an experienced gleaner. She leads the way, and I follow.

I felt as though I was picking my way through a bit of forest that I had never seen before. Her words were like another experienced gleaner walking alongside me to say, *There are strawberries down on the northern slope, or good mushrooms by the birches over here, or there is an easy way through the kudzu on the left.*

. . .

SHE KNOWS I'll find the strawberries. She points me in the proper direction and lets me *wonder* on my way over to them, feeling the already tested ground beneath my feet.

SHE SINGS, and her voice is like a song as sweet as silver bells. I feel the song go through me, and I hear the world bow around me, participating in the song.

She is like a dove who flutters over her nestlings. We sense her and open our mouths. Mouth to mouth, she sustains us as we grow. She nurtures and nourishes me again and again.

She broods over the world with a warm breast and bright wings. She is more intimate with me than I am myself. I am found in her embrace, understanding now, that I was never truly lost.

WE'RE IN THIS TOGETHER.
I will be your companion for life.
Now and forever, let's share every moment together.

THE LOVER of hover is hovering over me, humming and buzzing and creating still. Finding her reflection in my deep body of water has been my life.

OH, I do love you, Mama, Holy Spirit.

. . .

SNUGGLE IN DEEPER, *My dearest darling.*
   Indulge yourself in Me.
   Drinky, drinky, drinky.
   Stay love drunk.
   Indulge in the ecstasy of this Triune union.

MY LOVE IS AN OPEN DOOR. *Don't look to the right or left.*
   Find My face in your own.
   The light of My eyes will guide you and keep you.
   Let everything else go that tries to define you.
   You are perfect.

SHE IS the joy of all joys, the sustainer of joy, the nourisher of the Seed of Life. She is like glorious anesthesia that enables me to go through any trial.

She is the mother of many waters. Look as she hovers and gathers the whole world within her.

We are people of the Wing, and the Dove has breathed each soul into being. I can see her warmth and sweetness making me glow. She makes me giddy with pleasure and delight.

> *She is a gift to endorse our awareness of the*
> *Trinity abiding within us*
> *(see I JOHN 3:24).*

67

BUCOLIC BALLADS

*From him flows the original composition
and detail of our design. Like words
entwined in poetry, they connect layer
upon layer to complete the harmony,
following the rhythm of his thoughts
like footprints. Meanwhile, the body
thrives and pulsates with the energy of
love. Each individual expression finds
its complete measure there*
(EPHESIANS 4:16).

She writes with pleromic fingertips, dipped in rainbows, that lace her heart words with gilded grace and luscious love.

She writes books filled with light. She lingers on the details and the textures. She outlines Abba's dear face so all who read see.

Oh, how exquisite this will be. A phenomenon, an

anomaly, a masterpiece of his lovely face. She writes of the awe of likeness.

LET the record show that we are made in the image and likeness of Elohim. She's bringing likeness redeemed to real life!

SHE'LL TELL a story so vibrant and full of life that anyone who reads readily experiences life.

She seeks to unveil the love experience of Abba. This is the heart of her letters. She reveals a beautifully composed structure of a Man who gives life.

> *She is a Son-book, a Word alive to be read*
> *in every language, and God's spirit is*
> *the living ink (see 2 CORINTHIANS 3:3).*

She writes from Abba's heart, with intelligence and passion, to tell about likeness redeemed, innocence restored, and Union.

THE WORD BLOSSOMS IN HER, and she shines light over the beauty of the fields. Light beams from her eyes and ears, and nostrils and mouth. The dawn of exceeding brightness radiates through her heart and into her words. The Risen Son is shining in her letters. See?

. . .

SHE IS A ROMANTIC, a poetess, writing of the ecstasy and rapture of love. She writes of love, always love. Love, and only love, is her subject.

THE FULLNESS of his love has filled her, and she's oozing on the pages. She speaks a super sensual language that can be felt by heart. She is a woman of high imagination and creative fantasy, all for love. She lives in Love's face, oh lovely face.

HER SUBJECT IS majestic and adorable love, but it's more tangible than the ground your feet are on. It's a love holding us together in minute and magnificent detail.

THE CORE of her message is love. She is a love mystic. She dwells on the enjoyment of being so loved. Her panting heart has found her blue-eyed river of life, and she is enthralled with drinking and thinking of love.

SHE POSSESSES an extraordinary power with words, an intensity of seeing and feeling. All the senses come into play in her love musings. She seizes hearts and inspires imaginations and endorses likeness redeemed and innocence restored.

. . .

SHE LIVES in the Scriptorium of his heart. A beautiful place that smells of eternal Words and living epistles.

Day-to-day pours forth speech, fresh and mind-full of likeness redeemed and innocence restored. Words of life pour forth like beams of love lighting her reader's face like the Son.

JUST THE THOUGHT of being loved, and her pen stirs with a new melisma, and she begins to chant a nuptial song. The songs, chants, odes, and sonnets come to her, and she goes with them on many raptures, delighting again and again in the ecstasy of love.

Her words flow from pure grace out of a loving, loving heart. There is no hidden agenda to change someone's behavior. Mama Holy Spirit in the words moves hearts.

SHE WRITES poems on the indwelling fullness of the innermost Trinity. This pleromic poetry marvels at the fullness of the Godhead abiding and basking in our temples.

HER WORDS REMIND people who they are. They are keepers of memory, opening doors that seem to have been forgotten.

· · ·

SHE LOVES the Good Book only because it points to the beautiful Trinity alive inside of all. It speaks of a love story that would go to any length to restore Union in our fallen minds. So she writes of the fullness of God filling everyone. See now how her pen has grown arms and holds the whole world.

SHE READS the Scripture to see how wonderful she is. She is raptured not to escape this world but to live life deeper, fuller, and richer in it!

Her ink glistens with waves of love rising from the Scriptorium of his heart and stings her eyes. The strokes of her pen glow in the Son's light and shine like little faces branding their features on her heart's eye.

Her words ushered her into a world that can only be seen and felt by children, unscathed by disappointment and fear.

SHE IS AN AUTHOR BY ASSOCIATION. Before the fall of the world, the Author of the creation associated her into himself.

SHE GAINS WISDOM, stories, discoveries, and mysteries every time she beholds the beauty of his face. One brush of the touch of his hand, and she writes another volume on the plentitude of Abba's unconditional love.

Her script is alive and has a heartbeat. Can you hear it beating? Can you feel his heart beating in your chest?

SHE WRITES A PURELY poetic and bucolic book meant for grazing on in green pastures.

68

CONFESSIONS OF AN ECSTATIC

We are blissfully out of our minds with
pleasure before our Maker; he delights
in our ecstasy (2 CORINTHIANS 5:13).

E nvision nothing less than life in the fullness of our Union with the Trinity. Let this train of thought transcend and explode your mind with mystical union.

Soar with eagle's wings and experience the ecstasies of living so loved and enjoyed by Abba.

I HAVE BEEN LOVED into ecstasy and am experiencing a much fuller life now. Ahahaha. Love is the greatest ecstasy of all. It is the central ingredient for human flourishing.

. . .

CAUGHT in a river of his ecstatic love, with one look into his matchless eyes, I am immersed evermore into Him, who is pure bliss.

I live in the awareness that Abba really enjoys me. Who would've known that books could never teach what an ecstasy can reveal?

IN ECSTASY, in rapture, Christ reveals to me the ineffable beauty and immaculate detail of his face. It's the most marvelous thing I've ever seen.

I begin to see our similarities more than our differences. I see now that his righteousness is our common ground. That makes me misty-eyed, and I grin.

A little grin or giggle is all it takes, and I'm gone again, out of my mind and body, oh, this bliss of righteousness.

OH, heavenly Spouse, hold me in your arms. Even the thought of our marriage makes me swoon with joy and wonder (Mechtild of Magdeburg).

JESUS, you are my ecstatic lover. Those who feel the need to keep up appearances will frown upon these relations. I am ebullient and ecstatic in your love.

. . .

I AM ENTRANCED and romanced by Your ethereal beauty. Our hearts entwined give me Your insight. I see what You see. We stare together into a sea of infinite light, and I realize we are looking at the world alive and aflame in the love of Abba (Julian of Norwich).

THE PLEASURE of eternal certainty gives me wings. I can see the delight on Abba's face when I am sure of his love. This feeling is so joyful and full of goodness that I feel completely peaceful. I've got a peaceful, easy feeling, knowing I'm wholly locked in his eternal embrace.

I AND MY Beloved are on terms of intimate affection. He has created and destined me to enjoy eternal bliss and the light of his countenance. I have touched him, and he undoes me. Oh, the madness of this love. I am a fool for God and sometimes suspected of heresy. Ahahaha.

I FEEL ODDLY ILLUMINATED, transilluminated, as though the Son has found a place within me in this eternal life.

ECSTATIC IN LOVE, I am more interested in the monstrosity of salvation and intricate details of individual metamorphosis than the principles of tithing and fundamentals of evangelism (Pierre Teilhard de Chardin).

. . .

THIS LOVE IS IMMEASURABLE. I am plunged by love into the bosom of the deep and raised to the heights, carried to the length and breadth in Love's nail-pierced hands.

I BREATHE WITH GOD. His breath is sweet. My love has found me and bridged the abyss in my mind forevermore. Nothing can separate us, and I am undone.

ECSTATIC IN LOVE. Light is love, and I am drenched! We are love made visible. I am aglow with God. See the light?

WHEN HE HAD FILLED me with heavenly joy, he lifted me up and seated me on his Throne with him. I kiss the light of his countenance. He enlightens and mystically teaches me (St. Symeon the New Theologian).

IN MY UNDERSTANDING, I have already passed away. I died with Christ. I was already judged in him. It was appointed unto me to die once and after that the judgment. That happened about 2000 years ago.

Now I live. When Christ was raised from the dead, I was too. He ascended, and I did too.

.   .   .

I'VE DECIDED to enjoy heaven here now. I've decided to enjoy eternal life now. I've lost myself so completely, and I am rapturously beautiful in the light of the Eternal Son.

THIS UNIVERSAL AND enveloping embrace of Abba is both euphoric and ecstatic. Held in love, I am nourished and revitalized. He has persuaded me of his delight in me.

I AM high on the Majesty of the Most Adorable God and experiencing the ecstasy of our unhindered friendship. I feel myself established in love flowing from an eternal conversation of Unity.

69

MORE TO ME THAT CAN BE SEEN

*This will ignite your faith to fully grasp the
reality of the indwelling Christ. You are
rooted and founded in love. Love is your
invisible inner source, just like the root
system of a tree and the foundation of a
building. (The dimensions of your inner
person exceed any other capacity that
could possibly define you.)*
(EPHESIANS 3:17).

D rawn from wonder, she is the plan of Abba's
heart. The face of her birth has found her,
and he is pleased.

Face to face, she has found a beautiful space, and
she's not moving. Under his gaze, time transcends, and
she forgets her cares.

. . .

AWAY FROM THE coffin of religion, it was like someone opened the curtains, and there he was, smiling.

HER LIFE IS in perfect order despite her ongoing ecstasies with God. She's got time by the tail, so she catches it, holds it still, and enjoys the realm of eternity. She understands that eternity is the quality of life, not quantity. She enjoys being so loved by Abba.

She moves past the waves, the choppiness of thoughts. She enters the deep where sunlight penetrates in rays and beams, and nothing moves.

And she lives here, effortless and weightless, being One with the Trinity.

HER AWARENESS of being bound to Abba expands. She is dazzling. She is safe. She is kind. She is loved.

O FAIR SHE IS,
> *O rare she is*
> *O dearer still to me.*
> *Ye fleet and honied breezes*
> *To kiss her hand ye run.*
> *O fair she is,*
> *O rare she is*
> *O dearer still to me*
> (George Siegerson).

.   .   .

WHEN ARE we going to wake up? There are things we must learn, but there are other things that sleep inside of us that are already part of our inheritance. One of them is our ability to understand Union.

SHE WANTS things that most people don't notice, like living in lovingkindness and being nice to everyone. She wants people to feel important and famous around her. She makes people feel like a billion bucks, like they just hit the lotto jackpot.

She wants people around her to feel loved and valued, maybe even overvalued and overwhelmed by love. She wants them to walk away, scratch their heads, and say, *I feel especially loved.*

She wants them to know they are unique and beautiful just because of who they are. She wants to increase and endorse individual value, not diminish or invalidate.

VALIDATION IS ESSENTIAL TO HER. When people share their hearts with her, she listens to hear, not to tear down. She doesn't belittle their experience or give advice. She wants to share her grace space.

She's not here to fix anyone, just to love where she can. Oh, the astonishment of being so loved.

·   ·   ·

THE WORLD'S beloved faces are pressed into her mind. She sees Abba's face in everyone. He placed himself where no one would think to look: inside us, human beings.

She searches for the unexplored treasures of Abba in people. The world is a treasure chest, and each human is a fortune to be discovered.

SHE LAUGHS AND SOARS, propelled by rapturous joy so intense it verges on madness, and some will say, *She's lost it.*

She's a Pollyanna and hopefully optimistic, but it's reality. She lives in a real kingdom of love; some cannot see it yet, but she's certain they will.

MOST OF HER, you cannot see. She's inside this skin suit, but *the dimensions of her inner person exceed anything that could possibly define her* (see EPHESIANS 3:17).

SHE PONDERS much and reflects in her human senses how wonderful her soul is (Mechthild of Magdeburg).

SHE HEARS WITH HEART-SHAPED EARS.
    She sees without eyes.
    Speaks without language or tongue.

And Life has found her living so loved.

IN THE CORE of our life force lives a Face spilling free into every cell of our bodies. Oh, beloved humans, open your eyes and see his face in your face. The fullness of Abba's face is ours.

70

NUPTIAL SONGS

Speak Psalms to one another; burst out in
spontaneous celebration songs and
spirit-inspired resonance. In your heart,
do not let the music stop; continue to
touch the Lord with whispers of
worship (EPHESIANS 5:19).

Each time I sing, I feel the Spirit stirring inside my heart and guiding me. On the outside, I seem composed. Inside, I dance at the thought of Christ, my love. My face breaks into a grin so wide, you'd think I ate the Son.

HE IS the vein of my heart, Beloved of my innermost being. He is the Man of my dreams. He cures me. I always dreamed of someone who might help me, and he found me.

. . .

> *I am scented and in bridal attire. I know I*
> *stand before him in immaculate inno-*
> *cence (EPHESIANS 5:27).*

MY MIND HAS BEEN KISSED by love, light, and laughter. My forehead is marked with permanent kisses. I've been sealed with a kiss. I've got the mark of my bridegroom.

I AM the Bride of God. I have an inward flowering mystical awareness (Mechthild of Magdeburg).

OF MY BELOVED HUMAN BEINGS,
> *I open these gifts of ecstasy.*
> *Our salvation is a bridegroom in love.*
> *Oh, Your face has graced us.*
> *O Lord, it is over great that we are Thy love's mate*
(Henry Suso).

THE INTENSITY of his love for me holds me in a realm where only love dwells. Theology is not my strong point; love is, and I just keep writing.

I was excommunicated, and that was one of the best things that ever happened to my love life.

. . .

HE EMBRACED my soul with inexplicable love and united me to himself. Christ took me for his bride all before I even took my first breath. I have been in an arraigned marriage my entire existence; betrothed from the womb.

I WAS BORN A MARRIED BRIDE.

IN THE ROLE OF SPOUSE, he has granted my soul great intimacy. He inflames and consumes me with fire so agreeable and pleasant that it's impossible to describe it (Mechtild of Magdeburg).

HIS WORDS RING in my ears and give me strength. My speech is like music, so sweet and so free. He causes me to chant a nuptial song in a manner which delights him. Neither books nor studies can teach the language of this love song; it is heavenly and divine. It owes its origin to mutual embraces and this most adorable Word who fills me with his life and love by the kisses of his divine mouth.

The nuptial song is my soul's response to my well-beloved Spouse.

I AM A MINNESINGER. I sing songs of courtly love, bridal banquets, and sumptuous celebrations that include the whole world. I sing songs that mend; there are no subliminal messages of exclusion, separation, or delay in my lyrics.

I SING songs that call what I need into my hands. I sing rainbows into the skyline. I pause to consider whether I might find suitable comparisons in this world, but nothing can help me describe the embraces of the Word as he kisses my soul.

Kissing is in our future! I sing prophetic songs of kissing my Spouse.

I HAVE NO MORE DESIRES, for I possess my Beloved. He is, all in all, the life of all life and the love of all loves. Christ has taken us and made us wholly his. The worldwide bride is the object of his favor and delight and the heart of his own heart. This Union is ethereal indeed.

The bride is an orator of love, and there is absolute happiness as we speak of him. Christ has an uncontainable fondness for us, and we know it.

IF EVER TWO WERE ONE, then surely we
(Anne Bradstreet).

71

WRITING FROM A RAPTURE

R apture is a place of higher learning and immense beauty that transcends the language of indoctrination. There is no doctrine in a rapture. There are no fundamentals to be taught in an ecstasy. Rituals don't permit ecstasy or thoughts. There is no time for that in religious tradition.

In the rapture of Union, no mentality or reference to separation exists.

I LEARN by looking at the Triune face in the ecstasy of love. Pleasant is the theme that falls to my care while my spirit sheds light from the Son on the secret places of the kingdom, which is also my temple.

I am deeply affected by the hand of Jesus and inebriated in love.

. . .

I WITHDRAW *like one drunk from noble wine and lie down with benevolent feelings* (Mechtild of Magdeburg).

AHAHAHAHAHHAHAHAAHAHA.

Oh, blissful awareness of love divine. The light of Christ fills my mind with beauty beyond imagery as if I've tasted something out of this world. I am not drunk as you suppose.

THIS RAPTURE HAS the flowering poetry of an annihilated lover, of one who knows her soul is saved by faith alone without any work.

Oh, the wondrous waves of the finished work of Abba, ever new and ever enchanting, wash over me effortlessly.

Having gazed, I have become without past or present, always and only One with God. I've lost myself so completely that I don't know if I am still human; I am Love.

SHE'S A LIVING RAPTURE, raptured by love. Her countenance gives forth rays of light after her secret prayer. Roses appear when she is near. She is free, and she sparkles as she moves about in a glorious manner (Clare of Assisi).

. . .

OH, the dignity of this minutest piece of dust that has been lifted up out of the mud and taken as a setting for the noblest gem of heaven (Julian of Norwich).

72

PAPA

The Father himself is so fond of you and is
pleased with your affection for me
(Jesus) and your belief that I proceeded
from his immediate presence
(JOHN 16:27)

O sweet child of Mine, all Mine. I will hold you until you believe what I know about you. I will never stop calling you Beloved.

My Precious, enjoy being held. Nothing can match the extravagance of My thoughts towards you.

WHO IS GENTLER THAN PAPA? Is anyone more merciful and tender? He has found a place to put his tender heart inside of mankind.

. . .

Tell me again of your love for us. How you know the hairs on your children's heads. How every detail of our lives is entwined with yours.

You are so affectionate, so tender, and gentle. You convince and persuade me of your love. You delight in me. You join your thoughts to mine so that I co-know what you know. You don't give me mixed messages! With you, it is always pure love.

I am free to live loved in your arms. Your stronghold is not based on my good behavior. I am free to pout and free to cry. I can express my needs and negative feelings.

Papa has wrapped an unseen chord around my heart, which can never be severed. I am rooted in love and born aloft in his grace. This is eternity, knowing his touch and talking like family.

I will always only bless you and multiply you beyond measure (Hebrews 6:14). All this time, I thought I was earning my own way, and come to find out, my Papa was behind everything!

.   .   .

HE IS THE MAKER, the Lover, the Carer.
He is everything good for us.
Everything exists and lasts because he loves.
It exists by love and through love.
He made everything that is made for love.
The same Love sustains all.

HE IS SO MUCH MORE than any particular church flavor or religion. He doesn't major on the minors.

He mostly holds me. That's just what he does. He keeps me forehead to forehead. My mind clears, and my strength is revived. Healing spreads through my emotions, and the energy of his love feels warm and alive.

The deeper I go into myself, the more I find Papa at the heart of my being. Hallowed life and holiness are woven through every fiber of my being. It is my I-am-ness, my nature.

I'VE GOT YOU, My little love bug.

I AM RIGHT NOW as I should be. My job is to be loved. Because I depend on Papa's resources, I don't care what everyone else is doing or what's happening around me.

PAPA KNOWS ME BEST.

73

LIVING WATER

*And he pointed me to a river with crystal
clear, living waters, flowing out of God's
Throne, endorsing the reign of the
Lamb. There will be no memory of any
curse! God's Throne, endorsing the
reign of the Lamb, will be the presence
in her. Mankind's redeemed innocence is
the central theme of the city! And they,
his bond-Bride, will worship him for all
eternity (REVELATION 22:1, 3).*

S peaking waters touched her lips from the
fountain of the Lord so generously. She drank
and became intoxicated with the Lamb. These
waters are sweeter than she ever knew existed.

Her eyes are enlightened, and her face receives the
dew. Her breath is refreshed by the sweetness of this

living water. It has a pleasant fragrance. She smells pretty.

THE WATER of sight runs into her dreams. She's like a child on the banks of the River of Life. Her expression ripples with wonder and joy at the fullness of life. She trembles at the richness and immensity of the gift of life that Christ has given to her. It's a very big deal.

SHE TRAVELS up the ancient river road beyond expectation and into sheer enjoyment. Suddenly, the running River caught in her roots, and her fruit infused with the life of the Son to become sweet nectar.

SHE HEARS the song of the River and recognizes it like a memory. Life runs through her veins, and she's ready to dance. Happiness bubbles up through her like a bright, personal stream. She erupts in laughter.

Life runs deep in her. She tastes the life within, and she sees something new.

ALONG THE RIVERBANK are twelve trees. Some have emerald bark, and others have sapphire. Sparkling fruits are hanging beneath their branches. When the sunlight touches them, they act as prisms reflecting and refracting the light of Christ, like effervescent rainbows.

Brilliant-colored flowers and plants abound along the shore, glowing with inner radiance. She touches a petal, and it shivers with life. It feels like lamb's ears and whispers of Abba's love.

There are reflection pools round every bend. She looks and sees *Another* within herself.

AN IMMORTAL LAND is in our roots. A River of gladness is irrigating us. The region is full of unconditional love and eternal life. An uncontainable, unrestrainable River of intoxicating delight is alive in us. We are ministers of the drink of living water.

THERE IS music along the River where love wanders. All day, she hears the waters sing and sigh.

All along the River, life is beautiful. It runs crystal clear, full of shimmering aventurine and adventurescence. Mankind's redeemed likeness and restored innocence is the theme of the River.

SHE DIVES DEEP, purple deep, into mystic Oneness. The river nurtures and envelops her. Immersed in the River of Life, it's hard not to feel loved or alive. The deep water reflects the night sky so smoothly that it looks like a mirror. She sees the cosmos and is a star. The love of the Trinity is swirling around her. She rides the endless waves of his love. She has never not been loved.

HERE, in endless time and space, in the center of Abba's love, the center of the cosmos, the center and being of all He is, we let go, surrounded, sheltered, and held by love. A sense of eternity overwhelms her. Abba imagined us with great pride, and her eyes twinkled with possibility.

SHE'S LEFT the shores of tradition, and the love of the River broadens her interior life. She sees now in ecstasy; the River has always been under her skin.

We live in a place of constant love, immersed and perfectly at home in Christ's indwelling life, continuously, seamlessly, and effortlessly One.

He is Living Water.

She thought she was in the River, but the River was within.

WATCH HOW THE WATERS FLOW. Watch how it heals. The deepest of wounds are healed and cleansed with Living Water.

She has explored every secret place on the River she can find. Her thoughts are entangled with its voice, running wild and free. There is no place the River has not been.

THE RIVER CONNECTS her to her Throne-Home. She feels peaceful and unafraid, knowing this deep attachment.

Sometimes, the River carries her a little farther than expected, and she marvels at the new paradigm wonders she's seeing.

In her hands, she feels the endless life and strength of the River, and she knows it flows within her.

PEOPLE of the River know how to relax and go with the flow.

WHO TURNS the rock into a pool of water for a million weary escapees and the flint into a spring of water? (Hildegard of Bingen).

74

THE GARDEN

I t's different in the garden now that she is awake. In all truth, everything is different.

SHE SEES a flower and cries and giggles. Believe it or not, she had never really seen a flower before until she felt Christ's life inside. She sees Him and herself and the cosmos beautifully united and always adored.

SHE'S like a garden in the eternal spring. Her flowers do not wither, and her leaves do not grow brown.

SHE TOOK up a bit of earth in her hands and began to sing a love song over it, molding it with affection and shaping it with tenderness. Suddenly, it's a tiny creature like a bumble bee or a furry fly, and it flies away.

She picked a flower and blew on the flower head, and the seeds shaken loose went up on the wind like sparks of fire. She loses herself in the cool of the day. She is like a laborless lily.

SHE SEES the Gardener and warms in recognition. They laugh with delight in each other, and in every piece of laughter was a tiny bird coming out to fly among the lilies.

The garden blooms with bliss. She makes her way around. Everything is tended to and loved. Nothing she could see was useless, lost, or wrong.

SHE HAS a little dove hidden within the pocket of her heart for pondering. She pulled it out and kissed it. It is a perfect thing in a perfect place.

She puts the dove back in her heart's nest and runs about the garden dancing, leaping, giggling, high and wild. Back straight and smiling, all the while, her heart is blooming.

SHE SMELLS of Selah flowers and lingering. She is mind-full of Christ, a lovely and essential addiction.

· · ·

SHE HAD to go where she could grow. She finds Christ in things that grow in the most unlikely places. She has the gift of growing things.

In the garden, there is room for new beginnings. Seeds that fall and are buried in the darkness find a way to sprout.

The soil responds to her touch. She can make things grow. It's what she loves to do and what she's good at. It's as though everything around her responds to her words and breath. We are in sync with each other, all in tune like a hushed chorus.

SHE HAS fruit out of season and flowers no one has ever seen. Flowers bloom from her fingertips. She brings sunshine and new growth everywhere she goes. The air around her is filled with beauty and alight with wonder.

Her sunflowers do nothing all day but turn their golden-haired, 1000-eyed faces to follow the Son.

The irises are watching her. They grow three times as fast around her.

SONGBIRDS ROOST under her eaves no matter the season. She meditates in the garden. The highest form of her meditation is leaping and skipping. Ageless and evergreen with love, everything in her is flourishing.

· · ·

SHE SPEAKS of the Gardener in terms of endearment.

He is my Close One, my Alongside One, my Mate, my Spouse, my Adorable One, and my Green Vine, from which all branches sprout.

HERS IS a love of wild things, of things growing free. She is a Garden Bard. She writes and sings of the poetry of life. To hear a squirrel chirp is a joy for her.

SHE SEES things that have yet to grow. A bud on a branch brushes her hand. Summer is in there, a ticking love bomb. Its casing is dull brown, but she sees the brilliant colors of blooms and blossoms in the bulbs.

UP THE GARDEN path she goes, for spring has sprung in her. Abba gives her room to bloom, and she does, weirdly and wonderfully.

SHE HEARS the Gardener's whisper.

One cannot break the love bond that binds you with Me, My Darling.

75

FLOWERY EASTER

And the one seated upon the Throne said,
  Behold, I make all things new! And he
  instructed me to write because these
  words are true and to be relied on
  (REVELATION 21:5).

I am Florida outside and a panhandle of Paradise inside.

I SEE A GLORIOUS, beautiful space of light and color unfold within me. I pen songs and verses of Oneness and belonging.

A beautiful new dawn has bloomed in me. I'm covered in flowers and abounding in succulents. I'm a feast of flowers and full of innocence restored.

Look at my flora. I flourish and shine and grow in every way.

Christ is the Guardian of the Flora. I am a divine bloom. This Incorruptible Seed shall perpetually bloom and blossom.

AGAINST THE ODDS of accusation and condemnation, I end up stronger and blooming all over. Never again to be under suspicious scrutiny. Enough of classroom heads, time for hearts-a burstin, in bee-loud meadows.

THE FLORA BLOOMS IN ME, and there is a Gardener in my face. I am a resurrection garden filled with hints of frankincense and myrrh.

Here, I've learned the language of butterflies.

I drop to my knees and kiss the ground. I know I'll grow things here. The seeds in my hand will become a bouquet. I call gladiolas, asters, and lilies into my near future as though they already exist in every color.

(DON'T BE TOO practical for romance. So practical that not one ounce of romance is in you.) Spontaneity is the language of love. I contemplate the loveliness of Christ's face in all. It pleases me so well.

I see with clarity the emerald in the waters, the green of the flora and fauna, and the freedom of the birds, all because of this sequestered inside seat.

. . .

I FEEL *his close-nestling companionship in my sequestering* (Gertrude von Hefta).

I am not so attached to activity that I cannot give myself to contemplation.

I AM BLOSSOMING-FRAGRANT, *unmixed true love, without rue and bitterness in a love so sweet and deep as the abyss. He is my sweetheart* (Henry Suso).

HE IS the Vine from which I bloom and blossom. Oh, the transcendent Vine that sustains and nourishes his immanent branchlings. The Vine is tender, and the branches are miracles. The secret of the branch is the kindness of the Vine.

Even the simplest things possess the rudiments of immanence, a spark of Spirit. God is everywhere, even in all that is most hidden.

THE AIR HANGS thick with violets and lilies. I ponder among impatiens and gladiolas. The impatiens bloom nonstop in many colors. Impatient indeed, and eager to bloom.

The air is warm with humidity. I let my fingers pass over wisteria vines, and my ears ring with giggles. I hear the ancient conversation of Triune love longing for us. All creation speaks to those who listen.

IT'S ALWAYS GROWING season for me. Once I left the religious pen, my world became a paradise of blooms to get a buzz on, and seashores became an elixir. Even the air smells archaic, full of wonder, imagination, magic, and laughter.

ABBA GROWS my love stories and garden griots. Each poem becomes a peony. My heart is a florist of dreams and poetry, and my book is a bouquet.

OH, author of priceless blisses. Oh, giver of over-rich rains, of I a tender, young branch, bent and drank ever so deeply (Gertrude of Hefta).

BEHOLD, Who is here!
I tap my fingertips to my chest and grin. My heart beats with Abba's. I am alive with all of creation. I participate with the land and bring new life!

O YOU, living fruit, you sweet blossom; you, my beautiful blossoming daughter from My Fatherly heart. I enjoy thy beautiful bliss. (Mechtild of Magdeburg).

76

DAUGHTER OF THE WING

*Now (in the light of what we are gifted with
in Christ), the stage is set to display
life's excellence. Explore the adventure
of faith...Familiarize yourselves with
every ingredient that faith unfolds! See
there how elevated you are, and from
this position (of your co-seatedness in
Christ), enlightened perspectives will
dawn within you (2 PETER 1:5).*

A pure and high vista has opened before us in the light! I've found an eagle within myself, and I soar. Excuse me while I kiss the Son.

All day in exquisite air, I am co-seated with Christ, my love, high and lifted up. I sail amidst the earth and heavens. Up in the dazzling blue sapphire skies, round and round in majestic air.

.   .   .

Fly, fly, fly, Come Sweetness,
  To the magical meadows and streams,
  To the goldenest place ever known.
  Abba has placed us in his Son.

I've found the secret of the wind of which I am her descendent. I remember what it's like to fly free. I remember my wings.

Anyone who has broken free from the grip of a controlling, crippling belief or enforced ignorance knows the sense of coming out into the light and the release of being set free to fly and explore.

My cage days are over. There are no chains on me. I've been entangled in the twisting strands of love divine forevermore, never to fall again.

I feel lighter. It is undeniable that I am not the person I was. Christ has lifted every heavy weight, and I am weightless and free. All the heavy lifting is over.

I have slipped the bonds of Earth and danced the skies on laughter-silvered wings. I sway, I glide, I ride, with never a care. I ride the cosmic tide landing in Love's lap (Arthur Osborne).

I feel like a bird all day. It's grand, and my wings are large. My captive breast is his love nest. My soaring is my sword. My imagination soars, unfettered, as I feast on thoughts of likeness redeemed and innocence restored in Love's lap. I've fallen in love with blue skies and emerald shores rather than learning in classrooms.

WHEN ALL IS QUIET, the wind runs across the sugary white sand, whispering of Abba's lovingkindness. He teaches me the language of the wind and wings. I am a perchling nestled into his bosom.

I HAVE the same freedom as the wind. Free and wild, I've caught the wind to anywhere. I elevate with windy words, full of updrafts and uplift. The air around me is thick with trilling.

The sky is so big and blue, I fly transfigured, do you? The wind blows in every direction today, and I can go everywhere!

In this high seat of enlightenment, spread your wings in Union.

ON THE MEDITATION *of heaven's wings, soaring aloft, I breathe imperial air of love omnific, omnipotent, and omnipresent. The air warbles as it flows and carries me* (St. Francis of Assisi).

. . .

I SING WHEN I SOAR, and soar when I sing. Wind song, wind song, softly, his words move through me. He speaks most sweetly to me. I fly beyond this world and into another, outside of time and space.

AT THE MID *hour of night, when all are sleeping, I fly into the warmth of Thine eyes. And you tell me of our love from genesis and before* (Thomas Moore).

THE WIND COMES and kisses my face lightly.
You are My daughter.
A daughter of the Blissed Wing.

OH! *I've slipped the surly bonds of Earth and danced on laughter-silvered wings;*
Up, up, up, delirious, burning blue,
I've topped the wind-swept heights with easy grace.
With silent lifting mind, I've trod.
The high, untrespassed sanctity of space
Put out my hand,
And touched the Father's face and kissed it
(John Gillespie Magee, Jr.).

77

ANNIHILATED LOVERS

T*here is no place where my Beloved is not flowing* (Teresa of Avila).

I AM AN EMERALD MYSTIC, a water sound mystic of the Emerald Coast. Into the crystal clear waters, I slip in which my Beloved's voice I may hear. Although it is silent, it is far from dull.

I SEE my original face in his. Christ is my own essence. His face gives me so much pleasure. He is my life. He is my love.

I AM SO ENFOLDED in Him. He has poured out his divine nature so completely in me (Mechtild of Magdeburg).

.   .   .

I FELT such a deep inward connection and satiation that it was as if I had other senses than outward ones. I wished to withdraw from the hubbub of the outward ones (Teresa of Avila).

I AM SO DEEPLY ENTWINED I sparkle and shine. Behold this mysterious brightness in which one sees everything (Catherine of Siena).

LOOK, I am so dear to love, so lovely to embrace, so tender for the loving souls to kiss that all hearts should be fit to break with longing for me.

One tiny drop of Me and all the joys and pleasures of this world seem small. I am swept away into the Good.

How completely I have been captivated.

How I have been deeply soul-touched at the sweet, sweet words of my Beloved.

All my sweet love that thou canst experience in this world is only a drop in the ocean compared with the love of eternity (Henry Suso).

DEAREST DAUGHTER OF MY DELIGHT, in Christ Jesus. Sweet Jesus, Sweet Jesus, Jesus love. I am in a state of pure love now. Ecstatic with love and singing in the thrall of rapture. I have found a place that transcends all else and is pure bliss. I am high on love. I feel union, and it is indeed bliss (Catherine of Siena).

SINCE LOVE TOOK *charge of everything, I haven't taken care of anything* (Catherine of Genoa).

SHE FILLS *her heart with image upon image of taste, scent, and radiance as the bride and groom mirror each other's qualities* (Mechtild of Magdeburg).

EVERY DAY, *I feel myself more occupied in him. Love freed me more and more of all imperfection until I believed I am perfect. I have given the keys of my house to Love* (Catherine of Genoa).

SO GREAT WAS *the feeling I had in that sweet union that it is not to be wondered if I was out of my senses* (St. Paul, 2 Corinthians 5:13).

YOU MAKE *me live without care.*
  You make me live without care.
  You make me live without care.
  I feel the tender touch of my loving God.
  It is well with my body.
  It is well with my soul (Hildegard of Bingen).

.   .   .

My members were fastened to a tree.
  I died to set them free.
  Oh, my rich, free soul,
  Oh, pure conscience, oh, unstained innocence
  Oh, free and united heart (Henry Suso).

My sweet diversions. I am never diminished in his sight,
only exaggerated in his sweet and bright flaming love. I am
a throne of delight, a bakery of the most delicious delicacies.
I am deliciously adorned in the garment of light (Mechtild
of Magdeburg).

Happy is she, who in joyous security shall take me by my
beautiful hand and join in my sweet diversions to dance
forever the dance of joy amid the ravishing delights of the
kingdom of heaven (Mechtild of Magdeburg).

Enjoying the sweetest of moments, each one holy. I am
ever pleasing these Divine eyes (Mechtild of Magdeburg).

Pure, clean mirror of Divine majesty and immaculate
innocence. O fair shining image of Fatherly goodness. You
restored the disfigured image of my soul (Marguerite
Porete).

. . .

SHE DIDN'T FOLLOW any of the traditional rules for religious life, which made her suspect to many. She didn't follow a pastor or submit to rules of enclosure. The interior movement of her heart illuminated her head (Marguerite Porete).

THE SOUL IS TOUCHED by grace, stripped of sin consciousness, and engulfed in divine love. She is consumed in the ecstasy of love. A flash of light, the twinkling of an eye, the mirror of simple annihilated souls. Annihilated by love, the pure, noble, and high love of the unencumbered soul. (Marguerite Porete).

MY DARLING, you have read enough. If you desire still more, then write a book yourself.

FOR LOVE RAVISHINGS:

Ecstatic Confessions: The Heart of Mysticism, Martin Buber.

For the Lovers of God Everywhere: Poems of the Christian Mystics, Roger Housden.

An Anthology of Christian Mysticism, Harvey D. Egan.

The Home Book of Verse, Various Authors, Edited by Burton Egbert Stevenson.

Love Mystics, for further ravishings:
    Pierre Teilhard de Chardin
    Mechtild of Magdeburg
    Hildegard of Bingen
    Francis de Sales
    Henry Suso
    Catherine of Siena

Catherine of Genoa
Gertrude of Hefta
John van Ruysbroeck
St. John of the Cross
Marguerite of Porete
St. Symeon the New Theologian
Marie of the Incarnation
Teresa of Avila
Julian of Norwich
Hadewijch of Antwerp
Getrude the Great
Beatrice of Naz
Else Von Neustadt
St. Francis of Assisi
Thomas Moore
John Gillispie Magee, Jr.
Gilbert of Hoyland

www.ingramcontent.com/pod-product-compliance
Lightning Source LLC
LaVergne TN
LVHW052015080426
835513LV00018B/2038